facebook
Memoirs

ISBN: 0692296166
ISBN 13: 9780692296165
Library of Congress Control Number: 2014917276
Black Phoenix Innovations, Louisville, KY

facebook

Memoirs

HOW I CAME TO
UNDERSTAND LOVE

RICHARD O. ROWLAND JR.

BLACK PHOENIX INNOVATIONS

This book is dedicated to my late father, Richard O. Rowland Sr., and my lovely mother, Emma L. Bender. Thank you both for showing me what true love is all about.

I would also like to give kudos to my incredible stepparents, Mary Pettus-Rowland and Chauncey L. Bender. Thank you for showing me that love transcends all obstacles.

CONTENTS

❧

CONTENTS

INTRODUCTION
Why Me, and Why Now?

⚜

You come to love not by finding the perfect person
but by learning to see an imperfect person perfectly.
—Sam Keen, *Thoughts from Earth*

What in blue blazes is this precarious phenomenon we call love? If any of you are like I used to be, you believe that the very idea of love is a myth. At one time my love life could be summed up in six words: I came, I saw, I cried. And boy, did the tears fall. Love indeed was not my forte. Sound familiar? The fact of the matter is, I was all cried out over love. I was dusted, disgusted, and terribly confused. Frankly, I wanted everything to do with love, and sadly she didn't seem like she wanted to give me the time of day.

Ladies and gentlemen, please fear not. I said all of these things just to let you know I am in no way presenting myself as an expert on relationships. I am a mere mortal, like many of you, slowly picking up the pieces and trying to figure out how to put them back together again. This book details one man's account of how he came to understand love.

How did I come to this incredible understanding? Facebook. It never ceases to amaze me how men and women prefer to use the walls of Facebook to express their joys and pains about the dynamics of their relationships. If there's anything I learned from these random outbursts, it's the following:

a) Both men and women are clueless about the true meaning of love.

b) Too many men and women are more interested in playing games than in trying to make their relationships move forward.

c) Most men and women never understand how to get past these games to enjoy real love.

For years I did like many of you do: I discussed relationships with my family and friends. If your experiences were anything like mine, you realized that some subjects and some topics kept resurfacing over and over again. Over time I grew tired of sounding like a broken record, but I knew I couldn't shut my family or friends out. It is my belief that every man and every woman needs to find someone or something he or she can talk to when the going gets tough. Thanks to a suggestion from a friend, I found the means to continue holding candid conversations with family and friends about relationships without having to repeat myself. By just simply posting subjects and questions on my Facebook wall, I was able to give and receive advice as well as feedback. Incredibly the comments came rolling in. In the beginning I wanted to be a blessing for everyone else, but in the end I became the possessor of an incredible gold mine that I wanted to share with the world.

Sadly, one out of two marriages ends in divorce, 60 percent of second marriages fall victim to the same demise, and most relationships end in breakups. We can attribute the failures of our relationships to many factors, but I believe the number-one issue is how well we understand love. The statistics are appalling, but I am not ready to say it's time to throw in the towel.

This book is about my thinking outside the box and thinking out loud for all to hear. Plenty of my family, friends, and Facebook friends are asking themselves the same questions I posed on my wall. Surely you have asked some of these same questions: How do you feel about your boyfriend, girlfriend, or spouse talking about your relationship to family or friends? What are we to do if we are unable to communicate with each other? Are long, committed relationships a thing of the past? Why do we make loving each other so hard? Can two individuals meet online, develop a relationship through e-mail over a period of time, and then fall in love after they finally meet? Sadly, I really don't know, but I have a deep desire to learn. This book is my attempt at trying to get this love thing right for us all. I am challenging all of you to think about love in a way you have never thought about it before.

My Facebook research included men and women of various backgrounds who trusted me enough to unveil their most private struggles, past pains, vulnerabilities, and concerns. These individuals were everyday people trying their very best to pursue happiness. Shortly you will see that some were achieving great success while others were struggling to reach their romantic goals.

In the end you will realize the answers to *why me, and why now?* Our love lives have suffered enough, and it is time to love bigger and better than before. As the pages turn, it is my hope that you ask yourself: why *not* me? Why *not* now? Every one of us deserves to find love. We all hold the keys to our own hearts. We just need to learn whom we can lend those keys to for a lifetime.

All right, enough is enough. Let's get to understanding this phenomenon we call love.

*I have used pseudonyms for all participants to protect their identities and to ensure confidentiality.

PART I
Personal Rehab

❧

1

Who Can I Run To?

There are no foolish questions, and no man becomes
a fool until he has stopped asking questions.
—Charles P Steinmetz

Richard Rowland Jr.

At this very moment, you may be contemplating whether you should pinch yourself or not. I would like to assure you that you are definitely not dreaming. You are awake, and yes, this is really happening. You did just read the title of my book, and yes, it did say *Facebook Memoirs: How I Came to Understand Love*. It is my hope that you gain a better understanding of the peculiar phenomenon we have come to call love.

Have you asked yourself yet, "How could anyone be compelled to find any advice worth mentioning, let alone writing about, on any of the social networking sites?" I am sure without a doubt that you have asked, "Why did this guy choose Facebook in the first place?" Believe me, when the idea initially crossed my mind I had to ask myself on several occasions, "Richard, *are you serious*?"

The first thought that crossed my mind was that I'd had far too many Heinekens at the bar; I'd drank far too much Conjure Cognac and pineapple juice as well as my special grape Gatorade and Ciroc. I would like to advise each of you to leave that concoction to the professional Ciroc drinkers like myself. After deep introspection I realized I couldn't blame it on the alcohol, like Jamie Foxx and T-Pain. My second thought was that I might have become one of the many victims who had been stricken with the digital pandemic that has spread throughout our society, rendering useless young and old people alike. Were these the initial symptoms of the debilitating virus CFC, scientifically known as chronic Facebook cytosis? This horrid virus tends to leave its hosts in a vegetablelike state, and the only means of life support is for the individual to be connected to the Facebook social networking site. The symptoms of this virus include and are not limited to changing one's profile umpteen times per week; posting hundreds of thousands of photos; giving a play-by-play of each and every move or decision one makes; and, last but not least, displaying too much private information about any and everything in one's life and one's friends' lives.

To assure myself I had not contracted this debilitating virus, I began giving myself an examination. There is only one true thorough check for CFC, and that is to detach oneself from every device through which one can access Facebook. Within minutes and sometimes seconds of the detachment, individuals who have contracted the virus will break into cold sweats, experience withdrawal symptoms, and then exhibit the symptoms mentioned earlier in this chapter.

On what I feared would be one of my bleakest days, I can proudly say, I passed my self-examination, and while I did break into a bit of a cold sweat, the other symptoms did not ensue. As my systolic/diastolic pressures lowered back to 120/80 and my cold sweats ceased, I was left pondering my predicament.

The question lingering in my head was, "Why am I so fascinated by this social networking site?" I had been introduced to Blackplanet.com way back when; I had also been attracted to Myspace, yet I couldn't seem to put my finger on why Facebook held such a draw for me. After what seemed like hours of meditation, but in reality was probably a few minutes, something hit me.

I had a friend who asked me a very nonprofound question that ended up having a profound answer. She asked me if I enjoyed the various people and personalities who made up my list of friends. At that very moment, I learned why

I loved this website so much: because I was merely an avid supporter and fan of the various characters and personalities I had befriended via the Internet. On a daily basis, I had access to droves of people's most intimate thoughts without my even breaking a sweat. There was no need for me to call upon the likes of Inspector Gadget, Penny, or even Brain the Dog. I didn't have to call Matlock either. People were actually posting their most intimate thoughts on their pages for all of their Facebook friends to see whether they knew it or not.

Facebook had started a reality soap opera that should have been named *As the Status Goes*. It became quite apparent to me that there wasn't a need for daytime talk shows like *Jerry Springer* or the *Maury Povich Show*, which my friends and I renamed *You Are Not the Father*. More people would spend time following the various posts on *As the Status Goes* than on watching the "who wants to date a grade D celeb" show, *The Real World*, or *College Hill*. While those shows were and are still very entertaining, Facebook one-ups them on one thing, and that is authenticity and reality. The aforementioned shows do entertain the masses, but they lack the real oomph that makes *As the Status Goes* so appealing. None of these shows, with their edits and storylines, can match real life, real drama, or true stories.

Who truly needs to watch daytime or nighttime dramas anymore when you can just watch drama unveil itself on your desktop or laptop monitor via the comments on other people's profiles and photos? I know for a fact that one of the draws of this website is that it allows its members to witness the fact that no one is perfect. It is quite easy to let the not so good, the very bad, and the dog ugly situations displayed throughout Facebook overwhelm you, yet it is not time for us to throw in the towel. Depending on your friends list, you can find a smorgasbord of status updates and comment sections filled with pointless banter. At the same time, you can find status updates and comment sections oozing with motivational quotes and positive advice.

Are you still shaking your head? Do you still doubt the relevance of Facebook? Well, if so, please get yourself comfortable and strap yourself in. You are about to take a journey in between the lines, beyond the gray areas, and south of the black and white situations, where only a few nouns, pronouns, and verbs dare to go. I am about to take you were no single average Joe has gone before.

Many of you may be asking yourselves, "How can a single man I don't know from Adam help me in my relationship?" Funny thing is I have been asking myself that very same question. I have been the counselor to both my family and my friends for years. It's as if I am some sort of superhero. Everyone runs to me as if I have a cape that allowed me lift them above the fray, the vision to see through lies, and armor that thwarts any hurtful words or wrongdoing.

✤

Richard Rowland Jr.

My fraternity brother, Hill Harper, states in his book, *The Conversation*, "The simple yet profound act of holding a mirror up to yourself can truly be a frightening experience." I believe that a lot of people have taken issue with Facebook because of this fact alone. The numerous posts, status updates, photos, and profiles are providing reflections of the society we live in today, yet many individuals take offense to people airing their dirty laundry for the world to see. From time to time my friends and I have had deep discussions on the subject of Facebook's content. For the most part, a lot of them have negative reviews of the material available to Facebook's members without any age restrictions.

My main argument has and will always be about the content of programming on television. Have you taken a moment and looked at the shows? Have you truly done your homework and analyzed what airs in the wee hours of the morning, during the day, and at late night? Some of the shows that are on now amaze me. Tonight take a minute and watch *The Cleveland Show* or *Family Guy*. If you find these hilarious, you won't get any argument from me.

My question is, "Is either of these cartoons healthy viewing for young children?" Without a doubt I am sure you would agree neither of them is, yet for
some reason we can find each on at times of the night when our children
are awake. By the way, before you get all puffed up and bent out of shape
because I name-dropped *Family Guy* and *The Cleveland Show*, please understand one thing: I was merely using them as examples because they are so
well known. I just so happen to love the racy material on both, but I am an
adult. I am grown, and I can pretty much watch whatever I want to when I
want to. Ain't that right, Momma?

However, I see so many parents leaving their young children unattend-
ed, watching cartoons like these and even some of the reality shows like
Basketball Wives, and we have the audacity to wonder why our kids are
growing up so fast.

I can remember how, when I was a child, I could tell what time of the day it
was by simply looking at the programming that was on the television. Early
in the morning, you could find the *Today Show* along with local news, and
as the morning kicked off you could find a number of talk shows like *Phil
Donahue* along with *People's Court* and Judge Wapner. At noon you could
expect to see the afternoon news followed by four and a half hours of soap
operas. Following those were the five o'clock and six o'clock news, which
brought us to our nighttime game shows: *Jeopardy* and *Wheel of Fortune*.

Then we were entertained by the many primetime TV series, such as *The
Cosby Show, Miami Vice, MacGyver, The A-Team*, and, of course, you can't
forget *Dallas*. As the day was coming to an end, as my parents sent me off
to bed, the ten o'clock news was on, leading us into the late-night comedy
shows of Johnny Carson and David Letterman. If you were like me, sometimes you would sneak and watch late-night television. You could find the
intimate movies like *Emmanuel* on Cinemax, which my boys and I titled Skin-
a-Max. Not to mention HBO, where you could watch the racy shows *Shock
Video* and *Real Sex*.

That is no longer the case, though, because it seems the rules have been changed just to gross a few extra bucks. With that said, I am still not ready to write off cable or the Dish Network because with the flick of the remote I can find a channel filled with positive stories, news, or just pure entertainment. It is quite easy to become consumed by some of the reality programs and the like, or you can keep surfing through the channels until you find the programming you enjoy and for which you thirst. Cable now includes an arsenal of educational channels, such as the Investigation Discovery, National Geographic, and KET, which stands for Kentucky Educational Television, for those of you who do not hail from the Bluegrass State. You can utilize this surfing strategy on Facebook as well, allowing you to find some very positive people, profiles, groups, and comments. We can't turn blind eyes to the many positive networks on television while frowning upon the advantages of social networks.

In many cases I have found Facebook to be a godsend. It is true that in the beginning, I had a negative view of the website altogether, like many of you reading my book at this very moment. As luck would have it, one day I was bored as all get out, left home alone, staring at my four walls. On this groundbreaking day, I decided to take a deeper look at the two thousand people I had friended, and the range of Facebook connections I possessed amazed me. Of course I did have quite a few friends who had negative banter on their pages; others were hosting the positive types of conversations I personally needed. After that day I began visiting my Facebook friends who held positive conversations on their walls far more than the other ones. Those moments of dialogue became advice to me.

In my opinion Facebook allows you to follow the old saying "If you can't get rid of your friends, change them. With Facebook's networking capabilities, you can befriend individuals whose ideals are similar to yours. Facebook allows you to connect with men and women with different ideas and beliefs. Who knows what they may teach you?

Nowadays, finding good advice can be like finding a needle in a haystack. Please note I am speaking on the topic of good advice. I am not referring to the garbage so many of us receive from our family and friends. I believe that advice is like opinions: both are like a-holes because everyone has one. For the most part, people tend to seek advice from their closest friends and family. While I fully understand that you may strongly trust these individuals, please take heed that advice from the people in your inner circle could be of the bad variety. You may find yourself asking why I would say such a thing, but let me tell you something: I learned this in the school of hard knocks.

In my life I have learned that sometimes good advice comes from the most unlikely people at the most unlikely times and in the most unlikely places. I am sure there are a number of you who have asked yourselves who this Richard Rowland Jr. guy is and why you should take anything he says seriously. I am not going to sit here and tell you why you should give me a chance, but I am going to say I believe that my research has given me some great advice for each and every one of you to follow. If there were a PhD program in counseling with an emphasis on relationship studies at the University of Louisville, this book would definitely be my dissertation.

Many of you have decided to put your trust in celebrities like Steve Harvey and Hill Harper, to name just a couple, and there is nothing wrong with that. But last time I checked, love is not commercial. Just because you are a king of comedy, it doesn't mean you are going to make your wife laugh until death do you part. I might not be featured on MTV's *Cribs* or ever be on the cover of *GQ*, but I believe I know a thing or two about relationships because I have been in a few. And I have seen quite a few crumble before my eyes. Just because God hasn't blessed me with celebrity doesn't mean I haven't endured a thing or two that has led me on the path of personal enlightenment. Being the coolest kid or Mr. Big Shot does not make you the most viable selection to explain matters of the heart. I am not saying this to disrespect anyone else out here giving advice; I am saying it because it is the truth.

During the exciting process of writing this book, I had the honor and the privilege of having an editor on staff at Bellarmine University read it. This extraordinary woman asked something that has stuck with me throughout this entire project: "Who is Richard O. Rowland Jr.?" The funniest and most humbling part is that she had read only one chapter of the book when she asked me this jaw-dropping question. Don't be embarrassed if your knee-jerk reaction to reading the cover of this book was also, "Who in the heck is this man?" If that wasn't your first reaction, I am quite surprised. Why? Because the editor from Bellarmine University told me people have to be able to put a face with a name before they will listen to you. As you can see, I totally disagree with this idea. I believe that people need to know what you stand for and what you are about before they listen to what you have to say.

If you want to know who I am and what I am about, understand that the answers to these questions aren't going to help you in any way. You didn't buy this book to try to get to know me. You bought, borrowed, or even jacked this book because you found yourself sick and tired of being sick and tired of not being happy. I appreciate the editor, with her beautiful but humbling words, because she made me acknowledge a fact that I very well may have overlooked when I initially took on this project.

For all of you wondering why you should mark my words, I hope in the end you understand one thing. Like many of you, I have loved, and I have been hurt. Like any other man or woman, I strive to learn something fresh and new about love each and every day of my life. Who says you can't teach an old dog new tricks? If that is the case, the old dog might just want to watch out because he or she might find himself or herself replaced. I think the problem is most people despise change. Well, ladies and gentlemen, it is time to realize that with each new day comes change. The reality we knew yesterday will change today, tomorrow, and even years down the road. The world is ever changing, and so are we. There is no need to be resistant to something that you can't change. Change is definitely an inevitable part of our lives.

Have you ever found yourself asking, "Why me, and why now?" Believe it or not, I have found myself asking this question on a number of occasions, and none stands out more than when I took on this *Facebook Memoir* project. The book came together with a mix of luck and God's grace. Don't get me wrong—I believe that grace was the deciding factor in the matter, but luck did play a major part. By the way, I am not saying I believe I forged the book by chance. Due to experiences in my life, luck has an entirely different meaning to me. Many of you are under the impression that luck explains an individual's good fortune or lack thereof. Contrary to that I believe a lucky person is one who labors under correct knowledge. How so?

I had the opportunity to enroll in the BJ Miller Institute at St. Stephen's Baptist Church. The institute gave me the opportunity to take a five-week seminary course entitled Movies, Media, and Music, offered by the historic Simmons College of Kentucky. The class's main focus was to explain how the three mediums affect our thoughts and beliefs. To my surprise, one of the movies we did an analysis on was one I had watched every bit of one hundred times or more: the great Tom Hanks film *The Green Mile*. On this occasion the professor took the spiritual blinders off me, and I was able to see something in the film I had never seen before.

In *The Green Mile*, Tom Hanks played Officer Paul Edgecomb, who has an affliction of his male parts. Officer Edgecomb's deep pain removes the passion in his marriage, but some way, somehow, he and his wife, Jan, are able to find a way to love one another deeply. Each of us could learn a thing or two from this couple. I couldn't paint a better picture of agape love if I wanted to.

Don't get me wrong—neither of these individuals appeared to be perfect. For example, Officer Edgecomb is a very bullheaded man who does his best to avoid a trip to his physician until one night when the pain becomes unbearable. He is of the belief that the doctor will only cause more trouble. Many of you can relate to Tom Hanks's character. Your relationship has seen better days, yet you have been too stubborn to seek assistance. It's on the brink of falling apart, and now, when all hope seems to be gone, you are ready to attempt to put the pieces back together.

In the movie, Edgecomb's pain becomes so overwhelming, he is forced to make the decision to see his physician as soon as the morning comes. Sadly, Officer Edgecomb finds out that tomorrow is often the busiest day of the week. On this day a bad criminal with a tattoo of Billy the Kid comes to the green mile. In the midst of commandeering the new inmate, two of Edgecomb's officers are injured; the inmate almost chokes another one to death. In an attempt to protect the other officers, Edgecomb finds himself in harm's way. During the scuffle he receives a painful blow to his groin. After the skirmish ceases, the officers place the new inmate in solitary confinement. Edgecomb is in so much pain, he lies face down on the ground.

How many of you have ended up like Officer Edgecomb? Admit it: you have been dealing with some issues in your relationship. You know something needs to be done about it, but you have been ignoring it. Some of you have been just like Tom Hanks's character, believing that getting outside help will do more harm than good in your situation. I am here to tell you that if you run to the right person, you will receive more help than harm. Many of you have been putting off dealing with your problems for quite some time, and now you find yourselves lying face first on tear-stained pillows. At this very moment, it may seem like it is time to give up, but I believe it is time for you to look for a miracle.

In the case of Paul Edgecomb, the unthinkable happens as he finds himself face down on the prison floor. John Coffey, who has watched the ordeal, interrupts the silence and calls for the officer. There Edgecomb lies, listening to John Coffey say, "Boss, I needs to see you down here." After a few moments, Paul gingerly makes his way toward John Coffey's prison quarters. Ladies and gentlemen, please understand this is no simple feat.

John Coffey is about six foot five, and he is every bit as solid as an NFL lineman. I am sure you remember how big Tom Hanks is. Fearfully Edgecomb moves closer to John Coffey as another prisoner reminds him not to go too close to the prisoner. As soon as Edgecomb is in striking distance, John Coffey does the unthinkable: he grabbs the unsuspecting officer and pulls him close, and it seems as if all hope is lost.

At that instant John grabs Paul's man parts, and some way, somehow, he ends up pulling the sickness from him before letting go. Coffey then has a seat on his bed as the officer stands there in amazement. The great pain he has been feeling has subsided.

To sum up the rest of the story, Paul goes home and has a discussion with his lovely wife as she cooks. She asks him about how his checkup with the doctor went, and he jokingly says, "You know how doctors talk that gobbledygook."

Jan continues to cook as Paul slowly walks up behind her. He begins flirting with his wife for the first time in quite some time.

Jan flirtatiously asks, "What are you doing, Paul?"

After he has her attention, let's just say they find themselves getting passionately reacquainted.

How many of you have found your relationships like Mr. and Mrs. Edgecomb's? For whatever reason you have lost the fire, and all hope has gone with it. Rather than dealing with the situation, you both have been going through the motions, ignoring your heartaches and denying your pain. I don't know why men and women expect to see different results when they continue doing the same ole things each and every day. More than likely if it didn't work for you yesterday, it won't work for you today or tomorrow.

For all of you who have given up and are awaiting a miracle, look no further. You don't have to wait for your favorite celebrity to write a book about how you should think like a man or have a series of special conversations to find love; instead you can find advice on love in the most unlikely places, from the most unlikely people and at the most unlikely times—and this is one of them. If you haven't realized it yet, I envision myself as your Mr. John Coffey.

Ladies, all men are not dogs, and fellas, understand that all women are not sugar, spice, and everything nice. I pray that as you read this book, I will reach you in the nick of time, just before you give up. I hope you will follow me throughout these pages and come to understand it is quite evident that who you run to is very important.

I am honored that you picked up my work and are giving me a chance to discuss how I feel about love. I promise you that in the end, my intention is for you to come to understand love as I did, through the lines and comments of a social network.

Like · Comment · Share

Richard Rowland Jr.

Don't get me wrong: I believe that asking for advice is a good idea. We treat life as if we are each on a one-man or one-woman team, but I believe it is the polar opposite. Life indeed is meant to be a team sport, but the questions we must ask are: Are we asking the right sources for information? And do we have the right kind of people coaching and advising our team?

When we ask appropriate individuals for their input, the odds of success go up infinitely. In many cases if you talk to individuals who have successfully gone through what you are going through, you can learn a thing or two about how they overcame and how you have the potential to overcome. Please pay attention to how I worded that statement. This point is very critical. I am referring to the men and women who have successfully made it over, around, or through the situation in question. What good is it to receive advice from someone who has never reached the mountaintop because he or she keeps stumbling on the same pitfalls? Could he or she possibly be able to turn around and lead you in the right direction even though he or she keeps making the same wrong turn at Albuquerque? I think not. While an individual who has been where you are going may have an idea of how to help you cope with the issues at hand, can he or she help you climb back out of the bucket in which he or she is still stuck? These are all questions you must ask yourself when seeking advice.

This is why mentoring is a great idea. It allows an individual the opportunity to see the world through someone else's eyes. By *someone else* I do not mean just anyone. I am speaking of men and women you can trust to lead you down the correct path. Let's be honest for one moment. Most if not all of us learn most in life from our day-to-day experiences. I don't know about you, but I know in my own life I have come away with many bumps and bruises because I wanted to experience X, Y, and Z for myself. Now I have assembled my own little nuggets of knowledge. I see no need for any of my loved ones or friends to go down the same rough side of the mountain. That is why I decided to lay my story out in print. That is why the men and women who responded to this great project put their experiences in print. Together we hope to help everyone learn from all of our mistakes.

At this very moment, I realize some of you might be thinking, *I am not comfortable with airing my dirty laundry to everybody*. Let me let you in on a little secret: I am not either, but I believe it is of the utmost importance that we find that individual or group that can help us learn how to love and be loved. In some cases maybe Mom and Dad are the best to talk to about the affairs of the heart. What if they aren't? I believe the book *Rich Dad Poor Dad* by Robert Kiyosaki illustrates that point. The book is about a man whose father had a great education and a great job, yet he died poor. On the other hand, his friend's dad, whom he called the rich dad, had no education. When rich dad died, he was very rich and left an abundance of wealth to his son.

We can attribute Robert Kiyosaki's success to the great financial knowledge he learned from his rich dad. Robert's father believed it was important to go out and receive a proper education, get a good job at a good company, and work there till retirement. At one time this was sound advice, but due to the economic changes of the 1970s, this was no longer the case. Mr. Kiyosaki is now a wealthy man because of the advice his rich dad gave him.

I know it is difficult not to follow all the advice the men in women in your inner circle give you. It may behoove you to get a second opinion from time to time, like the author of *Rich Dad Poor Dad* did. Robert never would have been successful if he wasn't open to accepting advice from his rich father. There is one rule of thumb I believe we can all agree upon: no matter where it comes from, what is right is right all the time. Even a broken clock tells the correct time twice a day. It is upon each and every individual to do his or her homework to find the truth.

Like · Comment · Share

Richard Rowland Jr.

While I was in the process of writing this book, I had the opportunity to attend a Saturday night church service during men's weekend, when Rev. Chris Campbell of Genesis United Methodist Church was preaching the word. His sermon was titled "The Manure That Men Endure." The lesson was so captivating to me because the pastor was expressing how no matter the individual's economic situation, social status, or material wealth, there are trials and tribulations we each must endure during our process of maturation. In his lesson he also explained that during these times of pain and strife, we sometimes want to throw in the towel. Unfortunately many of us like to bail and take the easy way out.

We all must remember the old saying "no pain, no gain." Instead of throwing in the towel, the reverend explained, we should look to those who have come before us, to see how they made it out of their difficult situations. In other words we shouldn't be afraid to seek proper assistance.

For the most part, people seem to learn far more from rough times than good times. While things are all sunny, people seem to lose focus. When things are on the brink of disaster, people seem to get a tighter grip on life and focus on the task at hand. If every day were perfect, when would we ever truly have that moment to achieve a breakthrough?

Like · Comment · Share

Richard Rowland Jr.

I believe that in the twentieth century, society lost a key ingredient—a quintessential element of young people's rites of passage. We can link this lack to the breaking down of both our morals and our family values.

In the twentieth century, there was a pushing away from growing old and wise toward Peter Panism, or the desire to be forever young. Is it me, or is it already predestined that from the very instant we are conceived, we are in a battle against time? No matter his or her class or status, each and every individual must grow older until death comes like a thief in the night and takes his or her breath away. Unless we die young, growing old is inevitable. It is just a part of life. Believe me, I don't look forward to having a bologna patch where I used to have hair. I don't want to have a hairline similar to a horseshoe or the M on Mega Man's helmet, but this very well may happen to me. Regardless of all of that, I believe growing old can be a graceful process if you live your life accordingly.

In past centuries people honored their elders and showed them deep respect. In African, Asian, and European societies, elder statesmen were important assets to society. Young men and women grew up listening to the many stories and parables these elders told. From these secular parables, young people were able to learn about the tumultuous road of life and why they shouldn't take it for granted because each and every one of our bright lights will one day burn out if we aren't careful.

One such story is the South African parable of stepping-stones, told by Jay Moon. It reads as follows:

> A story is told of a young man sitting on a riverbank, feeling discouraged since he could not swim across the river. An elderly man walked up, rolled up his pants, and walked across the surface of the water. The young man was in disbelief until another elderly man arrived, rolled up his pants, and also walked across the surface of the water. Eventually a third elderly man arrived and did the same thing. Finally the young man decided to try for himself. He rolled up his pants and tried to walk across the surface of the water—only to sink, and the swift current carried him away. The three elderly men looked back and replied, "If only he had asked us, we could have told him where the stones were placed so he could cross the river safely!"

I firmly believe we can still learn a lot from our elders. Nowadays many of us miss out on knowledge because we end up putting our older family members in rest homes. It is not my intention to call anyone out. As a young man, I watched my mother and father put their fathers in rest homes because they could no longer properly care for them. All I'm saying is that for the most part, each and every one of our senior loved ones have gone through a gauntlet of situations which we are now about to embark upon. I am saying they have an abundance of knowledge into which we should tap.

For instance, we are experiencing one of the worst economic downturns the United States of America has experienced since the Great Depression. At this very moment, hundreds of thousands of Americans are throwing their hands up and are ready to throw in the towel. Please don't be quite so ready to give up. In the early 1920s, the United States suffered the Great Depression. The stock market crashes of October 24, 1929, and October 29, 1929, sent the economy spiraling. October 29 is nicknamed Black Tuesday, and it marked the most devastating crash that the United States had ever seen at that time.

Oddly enough, this crash came during a period when real estate values were declining even though just four years earlier the United States had experienced a housing market peak. Does this feel and sound like déjà vu? Over time the United States' economy grew stronger, and we were able to stand on our feet once again. I am blessed to have family members who lived through those horrendous times, and their words of encouragement let me know that with a bit of faith and patience, I too will see the economy stabilize over time.

I also can't forget that older people have an abundance of experience when it comes to affairs of the heart. Many elder citizens have endured heartache, divorce, infidelity, and so on. I am sure if you name a situation, there is a more mature individual who has been through those harsh circumstances and more. We all seem to look at the older people as if they are senile and couldn't have a lick of knowledge to bestow upon us, yet that is quite the contrary. These people treaded the waters we are nearly drowning in now. Just remember one important aspect of this discussion: you can't honestly have a testimony without a test, nor can you have true knowledge without an experience.

Like · Comment · Share

Richard Rowland Jr.

My pastor, Dr. Kevin W. Cosby, told the congregation a story that explains how you can't have a testimony without first having a test so eloquently:

There was a procrastinating duck that lived in Canada. The nation was experiencing an incredible spring and summer. The weather was so sunny and beautiful. A cool breeze filled the air, blowing from east to west. The sky resembled a Vincent Van Gogh painting. A beautiful, blue backdrop surrounded the sun, and the skies were clear except for the few clouds that appeared every now and then.

Every morning the procrastinating duck flew with his mate and comrades to their favorite watering hole for a bite to eat. There, humans would toss the ducks food every morning before they went to work.

Day by day the ducks followed the same routine until it was time for them to take the great voyage. All of the ducks came together and were talking of the great trek ahead of them. All of the ducks were getting prepared to fly south for the winter except the procrastinating duck. He watched as his comrades and his mate prepared for the magnificent trip. The duck's mate explained that he might want to get ready to fly too because it would be time to leave soon, and if he didn't leave in time it would be too cold to fly south.

Although the procrastinating duck's mate gave him sound advice, he wasn't ready when it was time to fly south. All of the ducks left him behind. Even after the ducks left, the procrastinating duck relaxed and followed the same routine until the cold breeze began blowing. Then the procrastinating duck became a little nervous, and he had no one to ask for help or advice. His only support were the words of his mate, warning him that if he didn't leave in time it would be far too cold to fly.

Finally the duck got off his haunches and began his flight south. As he flew over the Canada-Michigan border, he felt the cold winds blowing from the Great Lakes. He kept flapping his wings, but the voyage was getting harder with every single flutter. As he crossed the Indiana-Kentucky border, the procrastinating duck's wings became weighed down by snow from the clouds above the Ohio River. The snow became so overwhelming, the duck could no longer fly. He took a nosedive. He landed on a rural farm where cattle grazed.

As the procrastinating duck sat, shaking his head, he was thinking about the words with which his mate had left him. If he had just listened and gotten prepared like all the rest of the flock, he would not be in the predicament he was in now. All the procrastinating duck could do was look to the heavens from where he had fallen and cry out for help. He was sure he was going to perish.

When all hope seemed lost, a cow began walking in his direction. To the dismay of the procrastinating duck, the cow plopped a patty on top of him. The procrastinating duck thought, *Oh my God. Not only am I going to die, but I am going to die covered in cow manure.* To his surprise, though, the cow patty was quite warm, and it began melting the ice from his wings. The procrastinating duck became overjoyed when he realized he had regained full movement of his once frozen wings, and he didn't waste any time at all. The duck quickly flapped his wings and flew down south until he had reached his flock.

His mate and all his comrades were amazed he had survived the severe cold. All of the ducks wanted to know how this amazing feat had happened. The procrastinating duck explained that sometimes the manure we endure gives us the right amount of strength to push on no matter how hard life can get.

Like · Comment · Share

Richard Rowland Jr.

As I said earlier, I am deeply honored that you gave me an opportunity to help you understand love. Come journey with me page by page, line by line, and comment by comment as we attempt to piece together what love truly is from average Joe and Jane perspectives.

Like · Comment · Share

Richard Rowland Jr.

Question of the day: how do you feel about your boyfriend, girlfriend, or spouse talking about your relationship to family or friends?

Like · Comment · Share

Tracy Richard, asking family members who are knowledgeable about strong, healthy relationships doesn't bother me at all. My major concern would be if my significant other was having a discussion with someone who doesn't have a clue about relationships. How can someone who plays musical relationships know how to help us achieve a successful monogamous situation?

The topic also depends on your mate. What it all boils down to is: is he or she going to be completely honest about how things are going in the relationship? Is he or she going to lie to make himself or herself look good? Is he or she going to tell the whole truth, or will he or she leave parts out? The only thing I worry about is my family or his family having biased feelings that end up with them giving me or the love of my life dirty looks.

Angela Tracy, I definitely agree, girl. One thing I have learned from my own life experiences is misery loves company. Sometimes your friends and family don't want your relationship to work out because it gives them the opportunity to spend more time with you. Misery always enjoys company. Also everyone has a different opinion about the size of your problems. Things that you are willing to deal with might not be things they are willing to endure. If you discuss a small problem with your friends, family, or associates, they may turn around and make the issue bigger than it really is. I believe before we begin to talk to people on the outside of the relationship, we must first communicate with one another.

Carmen I don't have a problem with my partner discussing our relationship with family or friends because I am an open book. I believe that in a relationship, everyone must be willing to share his or her thoughts and feelings. With that said, if I want to know something, best believe I am going to ask about it. Ladies and gentlemen, we all can learn a

WHO CAN I RUN TO?

thing or two from one another. Understand I do realize there are times when I am led not to talk with certain people about certain things, but I should be able to talk to my mate about everything under the sun.

Erica Now just wait a minute! When there are problems in my relationship I believe that this is our business. I have been a witness to relationships that fell apart because family and friends messed it up. How? People who are on the outside looking in can take make the simplest miscommunication bigger than it ever was to begin with.

Kendra You better preach, Erica. That is one of the main reasons why my marriage ended. I believe certain things should be kept in the privacy of your own home. I didn't marry my ex-husband's mother.

Like · Comment · Share

Richard Rowland Jr.

Kendra, do you think if your ex-husband didn't discuss private relationship matters with his mother, you all would be married today? Was his mother overbearing?

Kendra Honestly, Richard, I think we would, but this issue was just the cherry on top of a host of problems. Sadly I lost my temper, and I blew all the way up. Yes, his mother could be overbearing, but I blame him for giving her the keys to our relationship. He would take something I expressed to him in confidence as my husband and run and tell his mother. If I can't talk to my husband in private without him going to tell our secrets, how can I trust him? Ultimately, because of this, I saw no point in trusting him, and I ended up shutting down our relationship.

Like · Comment · Share

Richard Rowland Jr.

Kendra, I read you loud and clear. Did you and he ever discuss how speaking to his mother dissolved your trust in him? Did you explain to him how it was choking the life out of your marriage?

Kendra Yes, we did end up talking about this, but it was too late. The talk did help out a little bit, but the marriage was over. To this day he and I remain friends.

Michael In my opinion, talking about your relationship with friends and family is completely fine. In fact it's a great idea because each and every one of us needs someone to vent to. We all need someone who will listen to us. Also we need people who can tell us good stories, anecdotes, while at the same time giving us feedback we can use in our relationships. Some topics can be off the discussion board, but these topics depend on the relationships, the people involved, and the depth of the discussion—e.g., arguments, intimacy, secrets, etc.

Nakia This can definitely be tricky. I think what needs to happen is the couple needs to talk about what is open for discussion with friends and family and what is off-limits in regards to their relationship. I said this can be tricky because everyone needs some form of a ventilation system at some point. Having pent up emotions will not be good for the relationship either. However, we can't miss the most important thing. Our dialogue in the relationship should be up to par. Both parties should be able to communicate with one another before we speak to anyone else about our issues. For some reason we don't always do this. The thing we all must come to understand is that while we have put the pieces of our relationship back together, our family and friends may not be supportive anymore. This can come as a result of something we shared with them.

Jacklyn I don't think I could find it in me to get upset with my significant other for talking to someone about our relationship. I believe the problem could arise depending on whom he is talking to and what they are talking about. It's a question of maturity when it comes to talking something out. As a married woman, I should not go to my single friends and talk about my marriage woes. I believe it would be more beneficial to speak with someone who has been married for fifty years and knows how to overcome the ugliness and struggles that come along in any relationship.

Now, if we are not married, that is totally different to me. If he or she talks, it is whatever to me because we are still learning about the person we are dating, and he or she is learning us. I believe that intimate things should be kept private out of respect for one another. If a person reveals private things, he or she shows you how much or how little he or she respects you.

Vanessa This is a lesson I learned the hard way. I was the type of person who told my mother everything. I quickly learned that some things were better off left between the person I was in a relationship with and me. I found out that when you allow people into your relationship, they feel the need to give unsolicited advice. Also you have to be careful. Sometimes when you tell your friends about what is going on in your relationship, it may open the door for them to wonder what it would be like to be in a relationship with the individual you are speaking of. I know this sounds messed up, but it happens all the time. Let's be real. Not everyone who smiles in your face and says he or she is your friend is really your friend.

Jocelyn I hate this idea. I have a very big problem with it. The more people you let into your relationship, the worse things seem to get. When you do this, you are setting yourself up for a terrible finish.

Like · Comment · Share

Richard Rowland Jr.

Xscape said it best with their hit single *Who Can I Run To?* LaTocha, Tameka, Tiny, and Kandi hit a chord deep in my soul with this beautiful song. I can attest to problems arising in my relationship that left me contemplating the right things to decide. What about you? It is in these times of need that we all need to find someone we can run to, right?

I believe this question is very important, and every single one of us will have to wrestle with it. When times get rough, and all hell seems about to break loose, who indeed can you run to? When life, your job, your children, your family, haters, or even your significant other kick your behind, there comes a time when you have to seek some outside counsel. Yes, there is indeed going to be a day when you don't have all the answers, and you are going to have to ask the great referee in the sky for a twenty-second time-out, and if things are as bad as they can get you might request a full time-out. I am sure sports analogies aren't the best way to relate my points to everyone, but I do believe this one will be straight to the point.

Do you remember the great Michael Jordan? Hello, he was God's gift to basketball in the '80s and '90s. Can you say Chicago Bulls, number twenty-three? As great as Michael Jordan was, I believe there were two individuals who were monumental in his incredible success. I will not argue against you if you say Jordan's success was due to his incredible drive and his work ethic because indeed your drive and preparation are important to succeeding at anything you put your mind to. The Chicago Bulls were a dynasty not just because of the great Michael Jordan but because of their incredible coach, Phil Jackson, who was a player's coach and an incredible motivator. He had his team primed and ready to succeed, and because of that they won an incredible six championships. Phil Jackson was a maestro of the game, and he knew exactly when to call time-outs to cease the other team's momentum. He knew what plays to draw up on the whiteboard to help his team succeed during the game. There were many times we all expected MJ was going to get the pass to hit the game-winning basket, yet every now and then his supporting cast was given the opportunity to win the game. Michael excelled on the floor, but off the court he needed his father to be his advisor. He made mistakes along the way, but his father taught him how to be a better man.

Many of you have that individual that you can run to, and that is all fine and dandy, but you must ask yourself a question: is this individual who you should be running to in a storm? I don't think anyone would argue if you had a great Zen master drawing up plays for your life or your relationship. I don't think anyone would have an issue if you had a great man or woman like Michael Jordan's father to run to. Also, before we can do anything else, the first thing we must consider is how our spouses or significant others feel about our discussing our relationships with anyone else. We all must understand that not everyone wants family, coworkers, or friends in their business.

This very fact is based solely on individual relationships and the people in them. I learned that this topic could make or break a relationship. We see a great example of this in the Tyler Perry film *Why Did I Get Married Too?* In it Jill Scott's character, Sheila, tells all of her friends of the financial problems she and her husband, Troy, played by Lamman Rucker, have been having since they moved from Colorado to Atlanta. Sheila tells all of her friends that she and her husband spent their last dime to take an annual couples trip. Throughout the movie Troy expresses to Sheila how he dislikes the fact that her friends know their business; he becomes quite angry and lashes out at Sheila. To make matters worse, Shelia asks her ex-husband, Mike, played by Richard T. Jones, to help Troy find a job in law enforcement since he golfed with someone who could help. If you want to know what happened, I suggest you rent the movie from Redbox or check it out on Netflix.

I believe that this theme throughout the movie was very telling of how many men and women feel. Many individuals, including me, are very private, and we don't want our dirty laundry displayed to the masses. I, like many of you, fully understand that at times there is a need for outside mouths and ears, but many people make the mistake of bypassing the individuals with whom they are in the relationships. What is the purpose of running to tell Momma, Daddy, your homegirl, or your homeboy when you aren't going to take this issue up with the one you love? I deeply appreciate all of you who have bought my book, but I will share this next fact for free. Many of you don't understand that what we do in the dark will come to light sooner or later, and when it does it is usually not a pretty picture. We could avoid the issues that come about if men and women would talk to one another rather than someone else.

Tim Alexander's film *Diary of a Tired Black Man* is another excellent example of why you must be careful with whom you discuss your relationship. In the beginning we find the lead character, James, played by Jimmy Jean-Louis, reading his diary for June 20. This is the day he is supposed to pick up his lovely daughter from his ex-wife's house. When he arrives he finds his ex-wife, Tonya, sitting in the living room with three of her girlfriends. On this occasion he just so happens to have gone to pick up his daughter with a special someone he has been dating for a few months, and she just so happens to be a white woman. The black women in the house notice that James is cruising up with a white woman before Tonya has a chance to see her. Once James pulls up in the driveway with his guest, he and she begin flirting and finally embrace one another and kiss romantically, which sends the women into an uproar. Tonya then allows the negative outburst from her girls to affect her mood, and she feels the need to prove herself to her friends. As soon as James gets to the front door, we see a colorful example of why you can't run to just any of your friends for advice.

In the case of Tonya and James, their marriage fell apart because Tonya's girlfriends played major parts in the relationship. The major issue was that neither Tonya nor her girls had ever experienced the love of a good man. Throughout the film Mr. Alexander gives us the opportunity to learn how each woman's view of men became skewed. All four of these women believe deep in their hearts that being a strong man means he should try to conquer his female. James, on the other hand, is a great man who doesn't believe in bringing drama to the household. He believes his primary job is to take care of his responsibilities, which are his wife, his child, and his household. Due to their past relationships, Tonya and her girls believe that men and women are supposed to be in constant verbal and emotional struggle.

This is why they have the reaction they have when James comes to the house with his new love interest.

What reaction? As soon as James opens the door, the women hit him with a verbal onslaught from all sides. "Oh, so you got to go get a white woman, huh?" Tonya asks as her houseguests look on with attitude. To make matters worse, Tonya serves up another zinger for James. She makes the accusation that he is too weak to deal with a strong black woman.

James is taken aback by this comment and responds, "I am weak?" At that instant one of Tonya's naysaying friends chimes in and calls him weak as well. The saddest part about this situation is that James is the best man Tonya ever had in her life. He is a successful businessman who allowed her to be a stay-at-home mom while their daughter was young. He provided Tonya with a house, her own car, and freedom to do as she pleased. Yet because of their backgrounds, Tonya and her girlfriends are unable to see James as a strong black man.

This is why we all must be careful whose advice we heed. If we don't we may miss out on our little piece of heaven on Earth. In the end we can all end up like Tonya. She is left to put the pieces of her life back together alone because she listens to her confused girlfriends' advice.

This example demonstrates how discussing personal problems with your friends can be an issue. Now, if you are one of the lucky few to have the likes of a Dr. Phil or an individual at that level, well, I see nothing wrong with discussing your relationship with that person because I believe he or she is definitely someone to whom you can run. In *The Diary of a Tired Black Man*, we see a depiction of how many men and women discuss their issues. People tend to speak to individuals they are comfortable speaking to, but that doesn't mean they are the best for the job. Many of us seek out individuals who will join our forces and be our yes-men and yes-women, but that doesn't help us out one bit. In the end we add to the problem rather than fix it.

In the movie Tonya makes the mistake of talking to her girlfriends about her husband, who is actually a very hardworking and loving man. Tim Alexander does a great job of allowing the viewers of his film to learn about Tonya's girlfriends. We become fully aware that none of them knows what it feels like to have a good man in her life. They have come to the conclusion that a strong man should neglect the woman he loves. Tonya had had nothing but negative relationships before she and James became a couple, and unfortunately for their marriage she kept the bags from her prior relationships. She never understood that James was nothing like any of her exes who hurt her. Tim Alexander makes it quite evident that you have to watch who gives you advice on serious matters like matters of the heart. If Tonya understood who she should run to, she would be in a strong, healthy, committed relationship, but because she allowed her insecure friends to help her she is left all alone.

Like · Comment · Share

Richard Rowland Jr.

Using family and friends can be a valuable solution to many of our problems, yet neither friends nor family should be completely submerged in our relationships. For the most part, this can be a very dangerous situation because people who love you are very biased. We all know Loddy, Doddy, and everybody who loves us wants us to be happy. This, at times, can be a problem. When you are discussing your relationship with one of these individuals, he or she can very well take things a bit too far.

In my life I have found myself part of a situation like Tonya and James's. Once upon a blue moon, I went to school with this guy who happened to be in a relationship with this girl I knew. I had the great opportunity of working with her. In the beginning, as most relationships start out, all seemed to be well with the world, but out of nowhere it was going down the wrong path fast. During the entire ordeal, my male friend did not alert me of any issues, and all seemed well on the southern front, at least from his perspective. My lovely coworker, on the other hand, took it upon herself to discuss her relationship with her family, her friends, her boss, and even me. She had no problem discussing issues with anyone no matter how big or small the issues were.

This young woman, like the two women from the movies we discussed above, believed that involving her family, friends, and coworkers really wasn't a big deal, but unfortunately it was. She didn't understand there is a right and a wrong person to run to. Her parents, friends, and boss developed negative views of her boyfriend even though they were receiving only one side of the information. In more ways than one, she had recruited a peanut gallery that was fully aware of the ins and outs of the relationship from her perspective and was willing to pass a verdict while having only half of the story.

We all know it takes two to tango, and there are definitely always two sides to every story. There is not always a victim. I have learned from my many conversations with friends and family that we are all at fault somewhere along the way. We all have to be adult enough to acknowledge the fact that many times in our lives, the choices we make cause issues in our relationships. Maybe you didn't say something out of line to your significant other, but you decided to take what he or she said personally. At the same time, you may not have been physically abusive, but you decided to disconnect yourself emotionally from the relationship, causing your mate to shut down. The list can go on and on and on until finally the two of you have had enough, and the relationship falls apart. Each of you sits there pointing a finger at one another, but both of you are the blame.

After a while my friends had a pretty messy breakup, and all seemed great with the universe again. Then everything changed again. My lovely coworker decided that even though the relationship was over, she felt the need to divulge even more information to her family about her ex. As you can guess, most of the information was rather harsh and negative. And you already know the family outlook went from bad to worse. After a short month of being apart, these two individuals decided to reunite. The lovely woman's mother became distraught and was quite agitated because her daughter decided to go back with who she thought was an undeserving man. In her eyes he was the devil incarnate, with all power in his hands.

It is quite reasonable that we all have to blow off a little steam, but we must be very cognizant of to whom we are running. It is quite easy to get trapped in the rut of habit and run to someone you always have run to when issues arise, but I don't advise doing this with matters of the heart. Many times you think you are venting, but actually you are throwing dirt on your significant other. This mudslinging can have some insurmountable implications for the future of your relationship.

My two friends are now expecting their first child, and friends and family alike are dismayed. Many of us are left rolling our eyes and losing our minds because we know that the two of them have no reason to be together. At least that is the opinion we have developed as a result of the supposed insider information we received. I am sure we would have different and more balanced views if he were as free with information about his private life as she was. He and I are alike, so I feel him completely. There will definitely be an uphill battle that my friend will have to fight because his girlfriend has unknowingly created a band of haters with her loose lips.

You can cross your arms and roll your eyes all you want to. I really could not care less what you are doing right now. I want to make sure you don't overlook the diamond that is in the rough. By the way, you and your significant other can be that diamond in the rough. Social networking sites like Facebook can be used to kill time and cure us of utter boredom, but as you can see from chapter one there is some deeper content to be found if you have the eye and patience to find it. I believe that each and every one of you can feel where I am coming from. It is up to you to decide whether you want to be trapped in negative situations or found surrounded by positivity. Life and everything in it is what you make it. Every tool and everyone you need is just a click away. Each and every one of us has the potential to do the impossible if connected to the right people. I hope you fully understand the six degrees of separation theory and take heed. If you utilize your social networking skills properly, you can very well find people referring to you as a big bag of chips with the dip.

Many of our lives are sputtering out of control because we have been sipping from the wrong well. Honestly you cannot blame that on anyone but yourself. None of us is a child anymore, and we don't have to live by the "do as I say, not as I do" principle, as many of us were taught when we were growing up. The most important person to run to when you are in a relationship is that person. Now, if he or she is abusing you mentally, emotionally, or physically, you need to find a way to run away and never come back because you shouldn't be susceptible to that mess. I fully understand that times get rough, but you will have to fight for anything worth having. Many of us look for couples without faults, expecting them to be good examples, but relationships that have endured the test of time are the ones you want to mimic. More than likely they have had their shares of problems. As you stand there contemplating the right thing to decide, understand time and patience will help you make the decision not to take the wrong direction in your life. With faith and time, you will learn where to go no matter what lies ahead of you.

Like · Comment · Share

2

Love TKO

Nakia The saying goes: "there are no victims, only volunteers." I take that to mean if you stay in a bad relationship, you're volunteering to take harm from it. Well, why don't we look at this situation as a person fighting for love or his or her marriage/relationship?

Like · Comment · Share

Comments

Nicolay Wow! Nakia, I agree with you so much, girl. Men and women have to quit walking around with their heads down, like they are victims. They know that they are in bad situations, but on a number of occasions they just don't think they can do better. That is why they enlist for this nonsense. I can personally say that I have always looked at myself as being a victim of relationships like these. Now, looking back on it, I have learned one thing. Each and every time the only constant in these situations was me. After taking an honest look at it, I couldn't be angry with anyone else but myself. Why? Because I was the one who made the stupid choice to stay in the unhealthy situation. I think there are several different factors that made me stay around. Sadly, as I travel back down memory lane, I must admit that none of them justified my allowing someone else to use or abuse me. I deserved so much more, but I just didn't know how to let go!

In reference to a marriage, I think it applies in a different manner because to some, marriage is forever. To me the definition of marriage is "until death do us part." I am one of those people who won't run at the first sign of trouble and will do any and every thing to make it work. There are lots of couples who try counseling to make it work, and I believe that is making a conscious effort. Unfortunately there is a breaking point at which you have to worry about how healthy your relationship is. Of course I am currently going through a situation where I care deeply for someone, but I'm not sure if we will be able to work it out. There has just been too much hurt and anger throughout the years, and yes, we are both thinking about calling it quits. Sometimes you have to cut your losses and move on and stop being a volunteer for unnecessary pain. When you feel like your spirit or your being is slowly slipping away with each argument, dinner date, or outing, you know it's time to let go. Marriage or no marriage, no one deserves to be mistreated for any reason. If you stay because of guilt, loneliness, sadness, depression, payback, or whatever reason, understand it's not worth it. Life is too short to waste time.

Marica I can definitely see why you would look at it like that, Nakia. Everything has a process; it takes time to build a strong foundation and to build a relationship, so it's only right for it to take time for us to get out of one. In my opinion we should first fight for our marriages or our relationships before we let them go. It takes input from both individuals in the couple. Once either one has communicated the issue, it is up to both parties involved to ensure that progress is being made. If in the end changes are being made for the betterment of everyone involved, we have reached a happy medium. On the other hand, if we haven't reached a compromise or an agreement, it is up to the individual who has the problem to determine how much more he or she is going to take. The truth of the matter is people end up doing what you allow them to do. That is why, when you explain to an individual that he or she is hurting you, and he or she continues to do so, you should leave. Your not leaving sends the message that it doesn't hurt that bad. Whether you know it or not, you are telling your mate that he or she can treat you any way without any consequences.

The thing we all must realize is that people stay in relationships for a number of different reasons. Some don't want to be alone while others stay for children, security, or even financial reasons. If you truly love yourself, you will chase after no one. We determine our own worth, and if we don't respect ourselves how can we expect others to respect us? We teach people how to treat us. We have to set the standard. When we say something, we have to be willing to stand behind it. As the saying goes, "If you don't stand for something, you definitely fall for any and everything." That is something my mother and grandmother taught me. When people show you who they are, you'd better believe them.

Haven't you heard these words before? Being in a relationship is a choice, and you can choose to be a victim, or you can be the victor. When things aren't going right, and you've tried to make them do so, that means you must go to the left. If things around you don't change, then change the things around you. We are not promised another moment but here and now. Life is too short to be miserable. Besides, if kids are involved, they are products of their environment. Please be leery of what they see because they may just grow up and be something they've always seen. We are the examples, and we need to stop being afraid of leaving the familiar and start our own paths. Just because it feels good to you doesn't mean it's good for you. I hope this helps someone. Everyone might not agree, and that's fine with me. Different strokes for different folks.

Natasha Nakia, I know exactly what you mean. I agree with you to an extent. A person should fight for his or her love, marriage, or relationship if it is a healthy situation. My problem is when there is cheating, domestic violence, emotional abuse, or a host of other negatives that some people accept in relationships. In instances like these, I disagree with sticking it out because these situations can be hurtful to your future love endeavors.

Shawn L. Natasha, I concur. I think there is a thin line between fighting to make it work and remaining because you don't have the strength or self-esteem to stand up for yourself.

Nakia, I agree that we do live in a society where people would rather call it quits than fight. Statistics tell us that over 50 percent of marriages end in divorce nowadays.

Nakia Kudos go out to both you and Shawn, Tasha. If the relationship is unhealthy, nobody deserves to remain and be treated badly. The divorce statistics stand out to me. I believe that people end relationships too quick and give up when all it takes is a little bit more elbow grease to turn the ship straight. Of course this is all relative to each couple's situations and circumstances.

Shawn L. I think the problem is men and women don't know how to seek out real insight in their relationships. How can we do this? The answer is simple. Reach out to the seasoned couples you have in your family and at your churches. In my place of worship, I have a pastor who told me a very telling story one day. He expressed to me that he and his wife had been together for well over thirty years. Of course I was like, "That is so beautiful." He was like, "Yes, it is, but this beautiful scene of matrimony doesn't come without work." He told me how between the two of them, there were situations of cheating, drug use, craziness, and even time apart. Somehow, some way, this couple persevered.

As a man legally separated from his wife, I can attest to that. It does take quite a bit of work. If most of us were true with ourselves, we would agree that we don't want to put in those real hours' worth of labor to maintain a relationship or marriage. At the end of the day, it is all about maturity. Hopefully we all will grow up someday. The question we all must answer is, "How much growth have we experienced?" Usually we don't get the answer to this question until turbulent times blindside us in the relationship. If you and your significant other have reached a certain level of maturity, you can make things work.

Nakia Shawn, I know all too well what you are talking about. Through all of those trials and tribulations, I have become quite the mature woman. I am ready to make some lucky guy happy beyond his wildest dreams. I am not one of those people who are quick to throw in the towel. I just have to find someone who is not going to give up on me quickly. If we were all honest with ourselves, we would all agree that none of us are perfect. Taking that one step further, none of us will ever amount to Mr. or Mrs. Right. In the end everyone can relate to the following three situations: Each of us has just gotten out of a problem, is currently going through a storm, or has memories of past issues that are still looming in our life. The problem I see with most people is they have a severe bit of misunderstanding. Ladies and gentlemen, in order for you to have a testimony, you must first endure a test. This path of life we trod is a tedious journey that is a collection of winding curves separated by peaceful straightaways with their share of potholes. Nothing is perfect.

Jocelyn I really do see it as fighting for something you want. I don't know any couples together for fifty years who haven't been through it all. In my opinion I don't believe there will ever be pleasure without some type of pain, whether it is lying, having to be alone because someone has to work too much, cheating, lack of intimacy, you name it. Every couple has to endure their fair share of faults. Every relationship has its own quirks. I never could quite understand why people say love does not hurt. You have to deal with some sort of consequences and repercussions when you deal with family and friends every now and then. The question we all must answer is: what issues are we willing to deal with, and which ones we are not willing to endure?

Marissa I understand the message, but I don't agree. Each and every one of us is different. I know this may sound weird, but some people like heartache and pain. Some women like bad guys while some men let women walk all over them like doormats. What is even crazier is the fact that some people like the idea of letting people use them. I believe what it all boils down to is self-esteem. Some people don't know any better because all they know is abusive relationships. They have been hurt so many times that they now believe this is the way it is always going to be.

Tara I believe that this statement says people do only what you will let them do. The question should be: how do you change this situation while you are going through this mess? You have to ask yourself how you can say you love yourself if you subject yourself to something that seems to be leading you to a hurtful end. This kind of relationship will not have a happy ending. In my opinion this sort of situation is not conducive to creating a healthy, long-lasting experience. Do you have self-esteem issues you need to deal with? We all must come to a realization that love does not hurt, and we all must consider a number of questions in reference to what love truly entails.

Wanda I read this saying on a friend's status: "Think about how hard it is to change you. Now think about changing someone else." It's fine to fight for a relationship, but some people don't want to be fought for. Once it gets to that point, I agree that if one stays, they are just cosigning the BS.

Like · Comment · Share

Richard Rowland Jr.

"Being proactive is about taking control and ownership of your life. It is not about laying blame or justifying, which is what victims do. There are no victims, only volunteers." It was the great author of *Keys to the Vault*, Keith J. Cunningham, who wrote the passage we are discussing. I love this statement. The words are so powerful. I am fully aware that as with all things in life, there are always exceptions to the rule. I am not in any way trying to say there are not any situations where people truly are the victims. This statement points out the fact that many times in life, men and women choose to play the victim rather than empower themselves to take an alternate action or course of behavior. Ladies and gentlemen, the point is we need to grab the keys to the vaults of our own lives and take full control of them. Yes there are many times when circumstances are outside of our control, but we still have the ability to make decisions. We all have stakes in this life, and we all have the ability to choose how we will respond.

We all have a very important question we must honestly answer for ourselves: is what we are experiencing worth subjecting ourselves to a little while longer? We must analyze this very pivotal question daily. Failing to do so could mean there will be some rough times ahead. If there is one thing I have learned in my thirty-plus years, it's that it's quite easy to get bogged down by situations in life. Because of this, if we aren't careful, life will literally pass us by. There will come times in our lives when everything seems to stand still, and let me tell you all a little secret: in these moments we are forced to see ourselves for who we really are. If that isn't eye opening, let me tell you in a different way. This can be hard for some of us to believe, but we are not Mr. or Mrs. Big Shot, like we think. Everyone you come into contact with may not know that, but there is someone special in your life who can check you for nonsense.

There will come a point in time when the high of the love spell will wear off, and the mirage of perfection will fade away. More than likely, after this ordeal, we will feel our fair share of jet lag. This should come as no surprise. I have yet to come across a man or a woman who hasn't felt the adverse effects of flying into a new time zone. Oh, don't look at me all confused and discombobulated. Have you already forgotten how high up in the clouds *you know who* had you until reality pulled you back down to Earth with the rest of us?

I must admit I still don't have a clue about this peculiar thing we call love. Some people treat it as if it is something you feel, see, hear, taste, and smell while others proclaim it is something you can do. I don't know about you, but I was blessed to have a mother who was an English teacher, and I learned how to use grammar rather quickly in my life. There is a difference between something we call a noun and something we call a verb. I hate to take you into the classroom for a moment, but bear with me. I won't be long—I promise. A noun is usually the thing doing the action, which is the verb. This profound fact brings me to a preliminary question we must address before we begin to tackle the subject at hand. If the noun is the thing doing the action we call a verb, then how in the world can you feel, see, hear, taste, or even smell love? I don't know about all of you, but I can say that none of my senses has ever registered coming into contact with this thing we call love. Even though my eyes have never seen love, my ears have never heard love, my nose has never smelled love, my hands have never touched love, and my tongue has never tasted love, I still have somehow experienced this so-called love business.

Many of us have been living our lives as if love is something we can pinpoint on our own personal radars. We each have to realize first and foremost that unless you and your boo have nicknamed one another Love, then love is not a thing. I know I can't be the only one who has heard those sweet words from his or her special someone, saying how much he or she loves you. Each and every day he or she tells you how much more he or she loves you, but sadly, for some reason deep down inside, you have to question whether or not this is true.

Why do you have to ask this question? Because talk is truly cheap. Love without effort is meaningless. In the very statement "I love you," the individual saying it is saying he or she loves you. Now wouldn't that mean he or she is proclaiming that he or she is going to do something to demonstrate how much he or she cares for you? At least that is what I would assume. I already know it is a bad idea to make any assumption. And I know far too well what happens when one is made.

I believe if an individual is going to claim he or she loves me, he or she must understand those three words together come with great responsibility.

What am I talking about? This great responsibility is a 24/7, 365 day a year job that has great perks and benefits but doesn't allow any time off. You can quit anytime you want to, but unlike any other job, if you apply elsewhere you start at square one each and every time.

What is the most important question the world hinges upon each and every day? OK, maybe that's an overstatement. The entire world is a bit of a stretch, but we can comfortably agree that a large portion of its inhabitants may very well base their lives on it. The question you must ask yourself every day is: is your love worth fighting for? Now, if you aren't in a relationship, of course this question is not for you, but if you are in the crosshairs of romance, you have to ask and answer this question daily. By the way, yes I did say the crosshairs of romance. Why? Well, it's elementary, my dear Watson. Love is a beautiful thing, but in the blink of an eye this beautiful thing can obliterate your hopes and dreams. I hope this doesn't scare any of you because I have always heard the saying "no pain, no gain." There is no reason to write off a relationship because of the fear of getting hurt. Now if you have been hurt, there is no need to fear getting into another relationship because you are afraid to get hurt again. Just because he or she cheated on you, it does not mean your next one is going to cheat on you. Just because he used you for your money or just because she was a gold digger doesn't mean the new man or woman in your life will drain you of your cash flow.

It is very critical that you ask yourself if this relationship is worth fighting for. I believe the very moment you say "I love you," you are agreeing there are going to be some rough times, and you are willing to hang in there just a little bit longer. I feel you are saying, "I am going to fight for this love to make it another day." While this might be true, understand that just because you and someone care a lot about each other, it doesn't mean your relationship will end in holy matrimony. So what if you and your significant other's relationship began the day after God said, "Let there be light"? This is in no way an indication that the both of you will be able to experience a healthy, loving, thriving, and beautiful marriage. You can have all the history in the world, but you have to be able to ask yourself if this thing is worth staying in.

Not only do you need to discuss whether the relationship is worth staying in; you have to ask yourself if the person you are with is worth fighting for. I believe this is where the problem lies. Men and women both have this complex that we have got to have what we want. Brothers are out there looking for women with perfect bodies and beautiful faces while sisters are out there looking for men with well-defined financial reports. Ultimately we have all become so selfish that we are out seeking men and women who will add value to our lives. People don't seem to get the point. Yes, these men and women should add value to our lives, but we too should bring something to the table. Just because you have the enchanting beauty of Zoe Saldana, the body of Serena, and the wealth of Oprah, it doesn't mean you are worth squat. Just because you've got the swagger of Muhammad Ali, the body of Idris Elba, and the bank account of any of the various entertainers who keep a steady line of work, it doesn't mean you're about anything. Sadly we all judge one another on outward appearances, leading me to believe the notion that men and women today are stuck on temporary things. I believe many of you are like, "Yes, my love is worth fighting for" until old boy doesn't get that great financial kick any more or until baby girl's body starts to droop. Then we leave, looking for that new temporary love.

How does this happen? Well, it happens because men and women are no longer seeking Mr. or Mrs. Right; rather they are searching for Mr. and Mrs. Right Now. When you love someone truly, you are not a victim; you are just a volunteer. You are not a victim because the fact is love is an option. People live their lives staring in the rearview, reminiscing about old flames and wondering how they let bad times occur. Well, ladies and gentlemen, how did it go down? I hate to be the bearer of bad news, but this happened because… Well, hello, we let it happen. Boom, I said it. You can't blame everything on what's his name or what's her face when you allowed yourself to stay in something that brought you no value. I have witnessed so many beautiful women who had it going on ending up with bad boys. I watched good men choose women who had some of the worst attitudes. In the end both the men and the women were hurt and left with bags and emotional bruises. This tempermental beatdown is not from a bully roaming the streets, pillaging unsuspecting victims for their lunch money. Unfortunately this pain was unleashed on you by someone you trusted—someone you thought cared about you. Keep this thought in the back of your mind. I will pick this conversation up while discussing how bags don't fly for free. As we mature there must come a time in our lives when we realize we reap what we sow. The things we allow to happen in our lives will have effects on us down the road. These effects could be positive or negative.

From the outside looking in, there seems to be far more losers than winners on the battlefield of love. In so many ways, it is as if men and women are experiencing a Pyrrhic victory, that's to say a victory won at too high a cost. Doesn't that sound somewhat familiar? Many of us have endured heartache and much pain trying to put up with you know who, trying to make the relationship work. Now, after all that time, he or she has come around. Do you feel victorious or a tad bit empty? Could the reason be you stayed around too long? You waited so long for him to cut up his player card or for her to quit playing games. Finally, after what seemed to be forever and a day, he or she recognized your worth. So you welcomed him or her with open arms. Sadly for you, the bitter days outnumbered the sweet days and left you unable truly to love this man, this woman, or anyone else to come after him or her. Why? Because you allowed yourself to put up with this mess for far too long. This is truly why each and every day, we must understand that loving someone indeed is a choice, and that is why we have to ask the question continually: is this love worth fighting for?

In the very song this was chapter was named after, "Love TKO," Teddy Pendergrass soulfully touches upon some ill feelings that many men and women muster toward the idea of love. As I already pointed out earlier, many of you have been emotionally beaten down a time or two, and now you are left wondering what you are going to do. Many of you are still stuck on something that happened to you in 1990, but last time I checked 2015 is upon us. By the time you read these words, it may possibly be in full bloom. You are still looking back over your years, reminiscing about all of the pain you felt, yet you stayed around, telling yourself that this time you would win. I believe it would be a wise decision to study the magnificent words of this song. In "Love TKO" Teddy Pendergrass sings about how he has been travelling down memory lane through many years. In the process he's come back to some times when he shed some tears. Mr. Pendergrass does something we all can learn from. The brother doesn't put his head down and his hands up in the air in despair. No, not this guy. Instead he uses this moment of reflection as a means of learning lessons from past situations. In the end he makes the decision to tell himself time and time again that this time he will win. That is something we all must do. David Schwartz, the author of *The Magic of Thinking Big*, eloquently explains, "Thoughts, positive or negative, grow stronger when fertilized with constant repetition." So that means it is imperative that you think positive and believe this time you can win.

The opening words of this song are something to which we can all relate. Evidently the man has been through a thing or two. And we can infer this from how he states he is looking back over the years, back over his life. Just as love is a peculiar thing, so is life, for we can't live in the rearview. Many of you are stuck in yesterday, just like Teddy P., and each and every day you don't ask yourself, "Is love worth fighting for?" Instead you just keep replaying that emotional haymaker she or he gave you. Some of you are so stuck on yesterday that you are looking at the mess and drama what's his name or what's her name took you through before you met whom you are with now. Clearly we are living in a Blu-ray era, but for some reason you are still trapped trying to watch old VHS tapes when no one has a VCR anymore.

This song is drenched in heartache that isn't happening in the present. This brother is reminiscing about something he already experienced. He can't claim the victory because he was too busy shedding the tears about his loss. Ladies and gentleman, look for a moment at the way the divine architect designed us. We were all created with our eyes in the front of our heads, and the only way to see behind us is to take the time to turn around and look. That is why carmakers make our vehicles with huge windshields and three tiny mirrors to reflect what is going on behind us. Last time I checked, as you drive down the lanes of life your primary focus needs to be in front of you and beside you.

In the second line of the song, we see that his walk down memory lane has caused him to turn a molehill into a mountain. How else can we look at the line "I guess I've shed some tears"? Hopefully you have taken the time to read the warning on the passenger-side mirror that says "objects in mirror are closer than they appear." I hear so many people justifying how hindsight is twenty/twenty, but sometimes if you overanalyze something you end up distorting what you were looking back on. Look at how Teddy Pendergrass does so. He doesn't say he *knows* he shed some tears but he *guesses* he shed some tears. Again, life is not to be lived in the past; it is to be lived in the here and now. There is nothing wrong with learning from past situations. The beauty of looking forward is you are able to get the big picture and see the things that are directly in front of you, and it is easy to see the things coming your way. If you spend your life looking in the rearview, you could miss a blessing. Also, if you spend your time staring in reverse, you may very well stumble on an obstacle you could have bypassed if you had been paying attention to what was ahead.

As you travel down the path of life you have to be fully aware of what is coming your way. I am not a firm believer in luck, but I do recognize that it is our responsibility to acknowledge when preparation and opportunity do meet. Life is constantly in motion. Living in the past can keep you from receiving your breakthrough, or it may very well keep you from your possible real chance at love. By the way, I am not talking about the reality show on VH1.

Many individuals have missed out on good things because they didn't con-tinually ask themselves if the idea of love was worth fighting for. When you love someone, you have to learn to forgive and forget. No, I am not saying don't learn from the situations; I am merely saying you can't find yourself harping on old news. Remember, objects in mirror are closer than they ap-pear. Whether you know it or not, you have the ability to create your sense of being. You don't have to let everything get to you. My mother always taught me to choose my battles, and I would suggest you pick your battles in your relationship. I have seen a number of relationships crumble because of argu-ments over things that weren't even the slightest bit important. In the midst of the arguments over some foolish nonsense, someone said something they really didn't mean and gave their significant others love haymakers that ended up giving the relationships love TKOs. This was not a result of the ill words that were spoken, but it was the beginning of the end.

"How so?" you may ask. Well, let me give you an example of how nonsense can end a relationship. Let's just say you and your significant other were hanging out in the living room when you had to go to the restroom real quick. When you came back, all was good. Later on that night, you heard a loud crash in the bathroom and a scream. Sadly you had neglected to put the toilet seat down, and your unsuspecting girlfriend's pretty little buns took a plunge into the toilet. You quickly got up and ran down the hallway to see what the ruckus was about. As you made your way closer to the bath-room, the door swung open, and there stood your lovely girlfriend with smoke coming out of her ears. At that moment you just so happened to let out a chuckle. As a result your girlfriend hit you with an onslaught of tongue lashes.

To make matters worse, you decided to join in the jousting, and both of you said some pretty hurtful things. We all know how arguments like these go. You said some things you didn't really mean to say, but there was no turn-ing back. You should have thought first, but instead you acted. Now you will have to deal with the consequences and repercussions, and so will she.

As the saying goes, there are four things you can't recover: the stone that has been thrown, the word that has been said, the occasion that has been missed, and the time that has passed. So please think before you say anything. In the end your relationship may be one of the many that fall victim to tiny spats that start over nothing.

This peculiar thing we call love is very delicate, and it requires quite a bit of attention, some patience, and, last but not least, some hard work. I am not a betting man, but if you show me a successful relationship, I am willing to bet you have two individuals who are working hard to make it work. In my life I saw a love I thought was worth fighting for die before my eyes, and it effects me to this day. My parents were married for eighteen beautiful years when finally my mother could take it no longer, and she dropped a bombshell on not only my unsuspecting father but me as well. My whole life I had watched two incredible people love one another. I never quite understood how someone could love another person for so long and just one day wake up and love him or her no more. Sadly, as my father lost his seven-year bout with cancer, I learned that you don't just wake up and no longer love someone. Love is an action you have to choose to do or not do every day. Every day you have to work at it, and every day you have to communicate. The instant you choose not to be open about your feelings or not to love him or her anymore is the instant your marriage or your relationship is not worth fighting for.

On the day of my father's funeral, my mother gave me a nugget of knowledge I will never forget. She explained, "Love is not something you can take for granted and expect it to work." She admitted to me that if she and my father had spent as much time focusing on loving one another and communicating with each other as they had building their careers, they probably could have made the marriage work.

Your relationship is worth fighting for if it is healthy. Honestly, when I think of a relationship worth fighting for, I think of a marriage. I am not saying your relationship with your girlfriend or boyfriend isn't worth fighting for, but I believe some relationships are meant to be seasonal. Some people you never should have been in relationships with in the first place. Due to this dilemma, you end up asking yourself why you are volunteering to have your heart broken over and over again. Have you ever heard the saying "love is blind"? In my opinion love is not blind. On the contrary I believe it is your lack of self-esteem that allows you to overlook the nonsense your significant other puts you through. In a relationship you and your partner both should be living examples of the golden rule. For those of you who are not accustomed to this phenomenon, the golden rule is the idea that one does unto others as he or she would want others to do unto them. Lately I've seen so many people doing unto others as they want to do. You don't have to take this ill treatment. If you don't want your love interest to give up on you then you can't give up on him or her.

A great example of this is in the movie *Fireproof*. This is an exceptional story of how each and every single day, you have to decide whether to fight for love or just give up and let it go. The movie is about a firefighter, Caleb Holt, who happens to be married to a nurse. Kirk Cameron, who plays Caleb, firmly believes in the fireman motto: never leave your partner behind. Yet when he gets off work, he is leaving his most important partner behind. Times are so rough that his wife, Catherine, is ready to file for divorce because Caleb doesn't seem like he cares at all. In our relationships we must have the mentality never to leave our partners behind physically, emotionally, or spiritually. No matter how hot it may get, no matter how tough it may seem, you two need to make the decision to endure the heat, especially in a marriage. I believe the problem lies in the very fact that men and women get stuck on Fantasy Island, and they don't recognize the possibility that the forecast of the relationship could call for rain. Every day will not be sunny, and you have to be prepared for those not so pretty days. All relationships have obstacles and challenges that will come along, but the two of you must be determined to make love work.

Love is in indeed worth fighting for, and in the movie *Fireproof* Caleb and Catherine demonstrate how something so beautiful one day can be hard to look at the next. They make the same mistake that far too many people commit: they blame each other for the downfall of the relationship, neglecting to accept their own responsibilities. Catherine's major complaint is that Caleb saved up a great sum of money he intends to use for himself even though he knows her mother is in need of some medical equipment for her home. Finally, with a change of heart, Caleb wises up and goes to his father for some direction. Surprisingly John challenges his son to a forty-day challenge he deems a "love dare," and Caleb unenthusiastically agrees. If you haven't guessed it already, this is problem number one. No man or woman can truly expect to succeed at anything with an "I'll try this out but don't think it will work" attitude. After all hope seems to be lost, Caleb wises up and discusses his situation with his father, who gives him a forty-day challenge called a "love dare." Caleb unenthusiastically agrees. This is problem number one. You cannot have an "I'll try this out, but I don't think it will work attitude." Don't you agree? If you don't, please continue to incorporate this belief in your life, and let me know how things turn out.

The love dare teaches that it is difficult to demonstrate love when you feel little to no motivation. Whether you believe it or not, love in its truest sense is not predicated by our feelings. Love is a divine expression of joy and optimism that is independent of circumstance. The mistake Caleb is making is the same one that is affecting a number of you reading these very words. You desperately desire for the relationship to work out, but you doubt that anything will make it work. If you have an attitude like this, you can't expect it to work. Once you have the motivation to do something to change it for the better, that is the moment when you can begin to turn the page. At first Caleb doesn't understand the lesson his father is trying to teach him. He follows the beginning of the forty-day plan as if it is a task, and his wife is very unreceptive. As he begins putting his heart into it, Catherine begins seeing changes in him and believing in them. Caleb and Catherine's marriage is saved because the love dare allows both of them to realize their relationship is worth fighting for.

I feel it was a good depiction of how you make and break your own decisions. The Holts' marriage is saved because Caleb knows who to run to. His mother and father entered a rough patch in their own marriage, but they found a way to make it work. Caleb's father experienced the forty-day challenge himself. His wife had to use the love dare as well to show him that she believed their love was worth fighting for. That is the nature of the beast we call love.

Is it worth fighting for? It is your responsibility to figure this out for yourself. Each and every waking moment, you have to decide for yourself if this is so. When you have a good man or woman, please do your best to cherish him or her daily. Love is not a one-sided thing—remember that. It doesn't mean you do things to get something; rather you do them because you want to let your mate know you love him or her. Love is not a feeling of euphoria. Love is not a feeling at all. Love is what you do. There is no need for you to sing any more sad songs. There is nothing wrong with love knocking you off your feet, but be wary the very moment love sucker punches you in the jaw. If you ever find yourself confused, remember this one thing: love is a choice you have to make every single day.

Like · Comment · Share

3

Do These Bags Fly for Free?

Richard Rowland Jr.

Almost everyone today who has experienced a failed relationship is carrying around some degree of emotional baggage. The problem with these leftover feelings is they are negative in nature, causing fear and doubts that carry over into future relationships. It's time to recognize our baggage and check it in order for us to succeed in relationships to come.

Like · Comment · Share

Comments

Darren Richard, you won't get any argument from me. That is the exact reason why I try to work constantly on me and my insecurities. That way I am not making any of these issues someone else's problem. It's not fair, and I wouldn't tolerate it if it were me.

Teri Badu In my own life, I believe that I am going to be charged high prices, like the airlines have done. I have way too many bags.

Kamesha Teri, I am definitely right there with you, girl.

Like · Comment · Share

Richard Rowland Jr.

Ladies, ladies, ladies. Just remember there is a lot of power in those bags. It was Thomas Edison who said, "If I find ten thousand ways something won't work, I haven't failed. I am not discouraged because every wrong attempt discarded is another step forward." Edison understood the value of perception. Sometimes when we believe we have made a mistake, we have actually learned a lesson. One of the keys to life is learning one lesson at a time so we can move onward and upward. I personally don't have a large amount of bags, but the ones I have weigh me down considerably.

Carmen Every day I try to start each morning anew. It is as if I never lived before, but I don't wipe my slate clean. The knowledge I learn strengthens my foundation for my next opportunity.

Shenika It is important for us to figure out which bags will be reserved for carry-on and which bags will be designated to leave under the plane. This may come as a surprise, but some of those emotional bags and past experiences we will need in our future relationships. Life's lessons can be drawn from these memories of yesterday. Instead of packing only the necessary things, like lessons learned from failed relationships, we end up overpacking. For whatever reason we end up bringing resentment, bitterness, distrust, and even anger along for the ride even though they are not needed. These bags make our future flights quite a bit more stressful than necessary.

Richard, you are so right when you say "check your baggage" because we all have it, and to some degree we all need it. This reminds me of being at the airport. Before anyone can get on a plane, he or she must first determine which items are necessary to carry along to go forward and which pieces must be left behind. In many cases some of us are lugging around old, worn-out pieces of luggage that need to be thrown away.

In the case of our lives, these are memories that should have been and need to be removed from our minds.

Jennifer Shenika, girl, you are so right. I also believe sometimes there are some bags that aren't even necessary for any of us to pack in the first place. What we do with these unneeded bags are solely up to every single one of us. I suggest that each of you reading my words pack wisely. It is important that you know which items will help you advance positively. You may find this to be a surprise, but sometimes the negative items from our pasts help us excel the most. It is up to each of us to decide how we want to deal with this. Make a decision on which items need to be discarded. Understand this takes a bit of soul searching, and it won't happen overnight. Please allow time for you to heal.

Jacklyn Bags surely don't fly for free. Everything comes with a cost. Take a moment, and imagine getting on a plane. What happens to each additional piece of luggage you bring with you? You are charged for each additional bag. At the same time, there are only so many bags every passenger can bring because the plane has a weight limit. I have witnessed people having to walk over to the counter to remove items from their suitcases to make sure the flight meets FAA regulations. That same practice is something you and I need to do in the real world, with our emotional baggage. We must learn that we must lean on a higher power to have this burden removed from our lives. Pray for your release, and it shall pass. In my life I had to recognize that the men I was attracting were weighed down by emotional garbage, just like me. At the time I didn't know. I was so consumed by the idea of having a man in my life, nothing else even mattered. Once I got down on my knees and sincerely prayed to my Lord and Savior, something magnificent happened. God helped me see what I was doing to myself, and in that instant I was able to release myself from those things that were slowing me down. Over time I will be completely healed during this release period. Closure is slowly coming to me. We all have to put our bags away in an orderly fashion.

Be sure to take the time to pull out all the negative emotions that resurface and properly dispose of them. Surprisingly this time has been rather smooth for me. As the men came back in my life, I felt like the woman R. Kelly talked about in his song "When a Woman's Fed Up." Fellas, there is definitely nothing you can do about it when she is fed up. Now I see these sorry excuses for men for who they are, and it's easy to dismiss them. There is nothing impressing about them anymore.

Like · Comment · Share

Richard Rowland Jr.

Ladies and gentlemen, this is your captain speaking. On behalf of the flight crew, let me welcome you aboard Romantic Flight 214 to the Rest of Our Lives with a continuing service to Love, Peace, and Happiness. We should touch down in the Rest of Our Lives at 7:06 local time. We have just reached our cruising altitude of thirty-six thousand feet. We are now travelling at a speed of four hundred miles per hour. I have turned off the seatbelt light, which means you are free to move around about the cabin. For your own safety, please fasten your seatbelt when you are seated, in case we encounter any unexpected turbulence. By the way, all of you who did not check in your emotional baggage will be receiving an additional charge. We will accept up to two pieces of this sensitive luggage with a maximum weight of fifty pounds per bag. Romantic Airlines realizes that at times, it may be necessary to travel with an item that exceeds the size or weight limitation or is in excess of the baggage allowance. Additional charges apply to this baggage. Emotional baggage does not fly for free.

What do we consider emotional baggage at Romantic Airlines? Emotional baggage is the stuff we carry around with us for days, months, and even years. It can be old hurts, resentments, feelings, or some kind of pain inflicted by someone else. It also can include carrying around guilt, failure, or some type of fear that impacts our relationships and life in general.

The thing we all must realize is that no mistake we make is irreversible. In many situations we are conditioned by the poor choices we have made and the horrid circumstances we have endured in the past. Sadly we walk away from these episodes believing any decision we make will be a bad one because of our past experiences. Ultimately, as a result of this thinking, we find ourselves in a vicious cycle. Thinking this way will surely have a negative effect on our lives. We become like Joe Btfsplk of the satirical comic strip *Li'l Abner*, who walked around with his own personal rain cloud over his head.

Why do men and women hold on to old feelings? People do this for a whole host of reasons. Everyone walking the path of life has his or her own personal agenda, wants, desires, and problems. Checking our emotional baggage is of the utmost importance. Neglecting to do so will result in some consequences and repercussions. Over time we will become comfortable—so comfortable, as a matter of fact, that we may die never being able to let go of the hurts, slights, and pains that are holding us back. Sooner or later we must break the shackles we have placed on ourselves.

Ladies and gentlemen, life is one long learning experience. Sometimes we are presented with undesired outcomes, and we think we have made mistakes, but in actuality it doesn't mean we really made mistakes at all. The key is to learn one lesson at a time so we can continue to move forward. It is hard to move forward while continuing to be fixated on what is behind you. It was the great inventor Thomas Edison thatwho stated, "If I find ten thousand ways something won't work, I haven't failed. I am not discouraged because every wrong attempt discarded is another step forward." Notice he said "every wrong attempt *discarded*." He didn't hold on to it. He let it go.

Many of us end up resembling chained elephants. How do you chain an elephant? The answer might surprise you: use a small chain fastened to a metal collar that is wrapped around the elephant's foot and attached to a wooden peg nailed into the ground. Incredibly this chain holds the elephant so strongly that the animal doesn't even struggle to break free. How does this happen? Well, it is called conditioning. The way to chain an elephant is to begin when it is just a baby. All you need to do is tie a strong rope around the baby's foot. The baby will struggle to break from its captivity, but eventually it realizes there is no way to break the rope and, even worse, continuing to try to break free creates a painful burn on its leg. As a result this baby elephant learns not to struggle, and it accepts that the rope or chain's limit is permanent, so there is no need to struggle against it. Over time the elephant does grow up into the most powerful land mammal, but it has a problem. The chain remains in its mind, and because of this the chain on its leg is never broken.

I know what you are thinking: *Wait just one moment, Richard. We aren't elephants.* Surely we know better than to fall into the same mental trap as an elephant with a chain around its leg, right? Wrong. Unfortunately, my friends, we don't know any better. We fall into this same trap all the time. It is not by choice either. Every last one of us was conditioned in an environment over which we had no control. So stop walking around like you don't have your share of emotional baggage because you do. Shari Schreiber argued that "everyone has emotional baggage; the question is, what are you doing to unpack that trunk and put it away, so your lovers, friends, and relatives don't have to keep tripping over it?" Please don't get your pretty little Vicky Secrets or your Hanes boxer briefs in a wad.

The fact of the matter is many of us are so caught up in the past that we can't focus on the present. Many of your relationships have fallen apart because you haven't let go. There is an analogy about catching monkeys that depicts this point very well. In some places throughout the world, monkey brains are a coveted delicacy. It is said they have the incredible power of increasing one's intellect and wisdom. The way hunters capture monkeys is quite interesting: They spread hollowed-out coconuts, with holes large enough for the monkeys to fit their tiny arms into, on the jungle floor. Then they place bananas inside the hollowed coconuts and tie them down. Once a monkey smells the aroma of a banana, it will come down from the trees above and place its hand into the coconut to grab the delicious treat inside. To the little guy's surprise, he will be unable to pull the banana out of the coconut. Still he continues to hold on to the banana. Even in the face of danger, this determined creature keeps its little hand wrapped around this banana, never realizing if it would just let go it would be free. This sounds crazy right?

Ladies and gentlemen, what is preventing you from letting go? Today I would like to advise you just to let it go. Take your hand off that old, rotten banana and begin loving and living again. It is time to recognize what emotional luggage we have and check it in. This is in order for us to have the opportunities to succeed in our relationships to come. Without doing so we will be stuck making ourselves go, no pun intended, bananas.

We have also got to learn to communicate with each other. I am not asking anyone to spill all the beans in the beginning of a relationship. I am merely trying to explain that if you want to build trust in a relationship, both people involved must make conscientious efforts. Notice I didn't say *try*. Many people never see positive results because they are still trying rather than doing. By the way, this may not feel comfortable overnight. It might not be easy at first, but over time the anxiety will subside. The great and world-renowned psychologist Dr. George W. Crane said in his book, *Psychology Applied*, "Remember, motions are the precursors of emotions." If couples work hard to build open lines of communication, ultimately they will communicate better. This may not be a field of dreams, but if you build it the trust will come. Talking to our mates is the only way we are going to break our shackles off our feet. Being honest with each other is the only way we are going to learn how to let that banana go so we can be free.

These conversations are important because men and women need to quit trying to put on these airs of flawlessness. No one is perfect, and no one was dealt a perfect hand of cards. I don't know about all of you, but there were times in my life when I did my best to hide my faults. I know what you're thinking, and the answer is yes, you should step out with your best foot forward. I am not saying step out of the house with your hair not done, your facial hair not groomed, or your clothes not pressed. What I am referring to is this notion that no one is going to love me for me, so I am going to pretend to be someone I am not.

Do you remember the first time you met him or her? You had everything in order. You took the time to open every door for her or to make sure every single hair was in place. All of us had this little game all down pat. Some of you still do today. In the beginning we were courteous, though if we were to poll friends and family they would say we were obnoxiously rude. We found ways to act selfless even though in actuality, we would do things for our significant others selfishly, hoping they would return the favors. Last but not least, we acted as if we were Daddy or Momma's angel, but deep down inside we were serpents waiting to strike our victims.

Everyone is guilty of this. I admit these examples are a bit extreme, but we all like to let our personal spokespeople speak for us. We spend so much time in the beginning of a relationship trying to keep up this front that we never give our significant others the chances to get to know who we really are. Like I said before, none of us are even close to perfection.

Have you ever met someone who seemed like he or she had it all together? Conversation was great, the time spent together was incredible, yet something was missing. I have experienced this in my own life on several occasions. Regretfully I also have done this to some incredible women in my life. Somewhere along the way, I picked up this idea that none of these ladies would love me for the real me, and if you were honest you would agree that is what you have done as well. We each have to learn not to underestimate our worth. I hate to be the bearer of bad news, but sooner rather than later our significant others will figure out the real you and the real me. By the way, that means we will have to check in some of that emotional baggage. I am not asking you to give an emotional dog and pony show, but I am saying get yourself in order. The love of your life will appreciate it. I would like to think you would be grateful for their being open, trusting, and honest. This will alleviate problems similar to what I have encountered in my life. People want to get to know you for the real you. Don't you want them to get to know you for who you really are?

I want the love of my life to love me for who I am. In order for her to know who I am, she must also know a little somethin' somethin' about where I am from. Too many times people act as if what was done in the past won't affect what is to pass in the future, and that is just a bunch of malarkey. I want to let you in on a little secret. This entire subject of emotional baggage is a discussion of how past situations continue to affect our lives. Believe me, I would agree if your argument were no one should judge you for your past. What has been done is done, but that doesn't mean your significant other doesn't deserve to know about it. You are still the same handsome man she thought you were even though you made some mistakes along the way. You are still the same beautiful and brilliant sister he thought you were before he found out you made some unsound decisions. I am still the same God-fearing man I was, even though from time to time I come short of his glory. All I am asking you to do is keep it real with your significant other. No one likes surprises. All right, I spoke too soon; some people, including me, love surprises. I just don't like that kind of surprise.

What kind of surprise? Do you remember the alien that resembled a huge cockroach in *Men in Black?* He was the alien that stole the man's skin and stuffed his body uncomfortably into it. Many of us are guilty of doing that today. No, we aren't out there body jumping, but we are masking people from the people we really are. We are hiding our personal agendas behind false intentions. The huge bug put up with this discomfort until he had accomplished his goal. We are all guilty of the same thing. Please take note of this. The brother from the other planet put up with masking who he was to accomplish his hidden agenda. His goal was to blend in with humans so he could steal the galaxy. He had to change who he was in order to receive something he didn't deserve. Does that sound familiar?

How many of you have felt cheated after dating someone you found out wasn't being himself or herself? I understand because I have been there on numerous occasions. Everything was all good at first, right? Sister was wearing that MAC makeup like there was no tomorrow. Brother was wearing that designer suit, and he was looking so sharp. Each and every day, you pinched yourself because you believed you had to be dreaming.

Well, baby, I got a surprise for you. You aren't dreaming, but you are definitely sleepwalking. This man or this woman has got you under a trance. In many cases these individuals don't mean any harm, but the results hurt all the same, and I know that pain all too well. Like the huge alien in *Men in Black*, these people have agendas to receive things they don't deserve. If they truly deserve your heart, they won't have to alter their personalities, dress up more than usual, or hide the emotional baggage they are suffering from to get your love.

Ladies and gentlemen, real love requires us to love someone for all of their good points despite their faults. That is something both my mother and my grandmother taught me. We have to stop seeking this Mr. or Mrs. Right because they don't exist. No one, man or woman, is perfect. Not one of us was born into a perfect situation. If something seems too good to be true, give it time. Sooner rather than later, the MAC makeup will come off, the designer suit will be hung in the closet, and the real person will finally stand up.

Richard, what is your point? Thank you, I have been waiting for you to ask. I am just of the belief that none of us needs to suffer the same heartache and pain Tamia sang about in her song "Stranger in My House." I am fully aware that over time, we all change, and that is to be expected. Hopefully as the days, months, and years go by, you and your significant other will grow wiser and more mature. I don't know about you, but I want someone to love me for being Richard O. Rowland Jr. and nobody else. It's hard enough trying to be the best man I can be. I want to love the woman of my life for who she is, not for whom she wants me to think she is.

Right now there are a number of you who have had your bodies snatched by aliens. On the outside everything looks up to par, but on the inside there is something more than meets the eye. To what am I referring? All of that emotional baggage that has taken control of your life. Deep down inside, your heart is trapped because you won't let go of all that old monkey business. What is the big deal? There is a possibility that your current relationship could fall by the wayside if you don't check in these bags. This happens because you are so caught up with what happened in the past that you are unable to focus on the present. Then you are doomed to keep repeating this vicious cycle. How soon you learn that the key to right now lies in your past determines how quickly you can check in your emotional baggage. Getting over it is all about being proactive. Refusing to be controlled by your past pent-up emotions is what will give you the freedom to take control of the here and now as well as your future.

How do you snatch your life back from your emotional baggage? I believe a self-evaluation is of the utmost importance. Before you can pack for the journey to the Rest of Our Lives, you must know all of the items you need. Once you have done that, you need to pack them. Now you are ready for the trip, but there is something you must do before you receive clearance to board Romantic Airlines. A lot of you have found yourselves in this situation time and time again, and you are still asking yourselves why you haven't been cleared to board the flight to the Rest of Our Lives. Ladies and gentlemen, it is a federal offense to try to fly anywhere without first checking in your bags.

There is a reason why these bags must be checked in. No, it is not another example of big brother keeping his eyes on you. The FAA has learned all bags must be checked in so there won't be any surprises that could have disastrous results for those who are on the aircraft. You know the routine. You decide which bags you are going to carry on the plane with you and which bags you are going to store in the belly of the plane. When you get to the airport, you drop the bags you want put underneath the plane at the baggage-check area. After that moment in time, those bags are out of your hands. You continue to walk to the terminal. At the front is an X-ray machine for your carry-on luggage and a body scan for you, unless you want to elect for the pat down. Now, at that instant you have to put your bags on a conveyor that will take them through the X-ray. Standing behind this machine is a man or a woman whose only job is to determine if what is in your bag is within regulations or not. If your bag checks out, you are allowed to board the plane. If it doesn't you will have some explaining to do, or you will be asked to remove the articles that don't belong. As you walk through the body scan machine, there is someone monitoring you head to toe, to make sure you meet the FAA's safety standards.

Another way to snatch your life back from emotional baggage is to check in all of your bags. You have to decide which memories you are going to carry with you and which thoughts you are going put on the back burner. Stop blaming yourself for things that happened in the past. Forgive yourself for the mistakes you made. Many of you don't mind checking your bags in at the baggage check, but you are afraid to check them in at the terminal. You have been unable to get off the ground because you haven't checked in your carry-on luggage.

I hear what you are saying: "What you talkin' 'bout, Willis?" I am talking about open and honest communication. Be honest; you have suffered a failed relationship a time or two because you and your significant other grew apart. Your relationship ended because, for whatever reason, you no longer knew the love of your life, and he or she no longer knew you. Somewhere along the way, something happened, right? She looked like the same woman you had fallen in love with before, but she didn't act the same. Everything about him matched the man you'd fallen in love with, but for some reason you just felt this couldn't be the guy you had been head over heels about. There appears to be a stranger in your relationship. How did this happen?

Many of your relationships suffered unnecessary growing pains because the loves of your lives accomplished their missions. They set out to steal your hearts, and you gave them up without a fight. Like in the movie *Men in Black*, the alien bug set out to capture the galaxy, and he was able to do so without a fight. Have you ever heard the phrase "beware of wolves in sheeps' clothing"? Well, beware of cockroaches in human skin. By the way, I am not calling anyone a cockroach.

I do believe that unchecked baggage can be dangerous to your relationship's health. Emotional baggage is a pest that can leave an offensive odor. Ladies, you may be under the impression that you smell good because you are wearing some Dream Angels Heavenly perfume by Victoria's Secret. Fellas, you may believe you are quite unforgettable because you happen to be wearing Unforgiveable by Sean John. I wish I could agree with you, but perfumes and colognes cannot cover the unpleasant aroma emotional baggage produces.

Ladies and gentlemen, you possess a perfume that is far stronger than any manmade smell. Song of Solomon 1:3 tells us, "Pleasing is the fragrance of your perfumes; your name is like perfume poured out No wonder the young women love you." I don't know about you, but I want my wife to find my fragrance pleasing. How will anyone get the opportunity to smell your sweet fragrance if you keep letting a pest taint your situation?

In verse three of the Song of Solomon, a woman speaks of how amazing her significant other's fragrances are. Notice she says *fragrances*. A lot of you are doing your best to cover up the offensive smells of your life. You have done your best to appear like you have everything together. For the most part, you smell great, but what are you going to do when that perfume wears off? Sooner or later that bottle is going to run out, and it is going to do so at the wrong time. In many cases the fragrance runs out around the ones you love the most, leaving them to smell the offensive odor.

You want the fragrance of your perfume to be pleasing to your significant other. That is why you have to do whatever you need to do to check in your baggage. Once you do so, you can rid yourself of those dangerous pests that leave offensive odors in your relationship. Once you have removed these burdens from your life, you will see yourself and realize you are a good catch.

Sadly I know this story all too well. Over the past five years, people have asked me why my beautiful girlfriend and I split up. After several late-night sessions of Facebook counseling, I walked away with the conclusion that my relationship ended because she and I started to be real. Are you familiar with the Dave Chappelle skit "When Keeping It Real Goes Wrong"? When I watched it, I laughed myself to tears. Now, comparing one of the hardest times in my life to the show made me laugh in order to keep from crying. What can I say? She was my one and only. She was my angel. She and I grew apart because over time we got comfortable, and our perfume literally ran out. Then we were both forced to smell our real fragrances, and it was quite offensive because neither of us took the time to check in our bags. It was interesting to me. Somehow the woman I fell in love with at first sight and grew to love deeper over four years became a stranger to me.

Looking back on that relationship, all I can do is shake my head. If there isn't anything you learn from this book, please learn this next point: knowledge is a very powerful thing when you use it constructively. I could have thrown in the towel and given up on love for the rest of my life. But I would rather choose to pick up the pieces and seek refuge at the potter's house.

I know what you're asking: "Who is this potter, and how can I find him?" Since we are all in different places in our walks of life, I can't tell you where you will find him, but I can show you how I found him. I didn't have to look for him high or low because my mother made sure I knew where to find him.

She already had a relationship with him, and she made it her responsibility to make sure I had a relationship with him as well.

One of my mother's greatest lessons was from a song, "The Potter's House," and it still comforts me today. I am here to tell you that even though you may have fallen by the wayside of life, you can take your problems to the potter's house. If your dreams and visions are shattered, you can pick up the pieces and take them to the potter's house. Why can you take your issues to the potter's house? The songwriter tells us, "You don't have to stay in the shape that you're in/The potter wants to put you back together again." You don't have to choose to be a victim of your past because he wants to prosper you.

We already established the fact that every single one of us carries around some degree of emotional baggage. We all have these pent-up emotions, thoughts, and issues, and that means we all have to deal with them. One thing I know for sure is that some of us make the decision not to be defeated by them while others become paralyzed by them. Some people have been dealing with their emotional baggage for so long they have developed what I like to call excusitis. This is a condition when men and women find all sorts of reasons, which are actually excuses, to justify why they haven't moved on. It is quite all right to sulk for six months. When you fall down and scrape your knee, it takes your body time to heal, and during this period you keep it clean and apply ointment to help it. The problem I see is that men and women act like it doesn't take time for an emotional scratch to heal. We all need a little time to get over our problems, but some of you take that to the extreme. Some of you are still wearing the same Band-Aid® from like six years ago, and the crusty thing is barely hanging on. Your wound has been healed for quite some time, but you are too stubborn to take off the blasted thing. Whatever the case may be, you still think your wound hasn't healed, even though everyone around you can clearly tell it is time for you to take off that despicable Band-Aid®.

Ladies and gentlemen, there comes a time in each of our lives when we have to take responsibility for everything we have gone through. We can't keep using all the mishaps we have gone through in life as reasons for why we can't move on. We already took the first step in our personal rehab, and we have discovered the right people to run to. I am sure what I am about to say will sound corny, but it is true. If your house were consumed by ghosts, I bet you would call the Ghostbusters. I mean, who else would you call? Are you going to call Keisha, Tyrone, Becky, Billy, or whoever else? Please enlighten me if they get rid of that ghost problem for you.

We have taken the second step: we have quit acting like we are victims, and we have accepted our roles in all of this. Now it is time for us to complete our journey. On our trip to the Rest of Our Lives, let me be your guide. When you take any trip, you have to decide what is necessary to take along and what is not. I would like to think none of you would pack a fur for a trip to the Bahamas. I am sure if you did something like that, you would be that random security check, and thank God for that. If you weren't that random check, I believe—actually I know—I wouldn't get on the flight because obviously the airline doesn't seem to have a safety-first attitude. We all know that an airplane's ability to get from A to Z is connected to the amount of weight an aircraft is carrying. Also there are certain things you can take aboard and other things you can't.

Life would be much easier if there was a personal guide to tell you what you could and couldn't take on your Romantic Airline. Many of your flights can't get off the ground because you are accepting any and everything on-board. Now, don't sit there getting an attitude, grumbling excuses under your breath. Remember, we just acknowledged that we aren't going to play the victim role anymore, and we are going to assume some responsibility for the situations in which we find ourselves.

Just think about this for a moment. Before you read this chapter on emotional baggage, you believed that your bags weren't costing you a thing. Are you sure about that now? I would like to believe you are sure. I suggest you get your packing skills in order and recognize what is necessary for your upcoming trip, which, again, is the rest of your life. I don't intend for this to be a temporary joy tour. I want this to be a permanent move. I want you to see me around in some city and say Richard, I am no longer on Dreary Island. I now reside in the State of Happiness, in the capital city of Joy. I want each and every one of you to drop those unnecessary bags and breathe much-needed sighs of relief. Ah!

It is very critical that we each pack appropriately for our trip. This is for your good. It is necessary for you to decide which bags you will put tags on and take to the baggage drop belt and which bags you will carry on, to be with you on the flight. The problem hasn't been that you are traveling around with baggage because we are all doing this. The problem is you are on this plane with these huge suitcases, and you put your duffel bag, with your magazines, iPod, and whatever else you brought to ease the journey, on the baggage belt. Now you and the passengers sitting next to you sit all cramped up, and it is quite uncomfortable. To make matters worse, you are bored out of your mind because you didn't select the right bags to carry on the flight.

I hope by now I have made it perfectly clear that the problem is not that you have baggage. Honestly I think relationships and credit have something in common. All of you who don't have any baggage, I must ask you: how are we to know what kind of relationship history you have? No one can get financing without credit because the banks are afraid. They aren't sure if you will follow the agreement you sign. The same can be said if you don't have any baggage whatsoever. None of us has to worry about this fact because we have established that everyone has some degree of emotional baggage. Second, who takes a flight without packing some luggage unless he or she intends on getting all the necessary things at the destination?

Many of our relationships haven't taken off yet because we haven't packed the plane appropriately. For all of you who are in the back of the line, understand you might have to adjust what you have in your suitcases and carry-on bags to ensure the plane is going to take off safely, fly, and then land at the destination. The weight an airplane is carrying and the amount of fuel it burns is connected. The less weight carried, the less fuel consumed and vice versa. Many of your airlines are wasting precious fuel on this journey called the rest of your life. Due to the intense weight, your journey has been interrupted by an emergency landing. Now you are stuck waiting for a rescue team to come get you.

Does that sound like anyone you know? Maybe you? Personally that was me for five years. The emotional baggage I took from my last relationship was so insurmountable that my Romantic Airlines repeatedly had emergency landings. The saddest part is that most flights didn't even get off the ground. I was so ready to go, yet there I was, sitting in my favorite window seat, waiting for the stewardess to shut and lock the door so we could take off. Then, like clockwork, the captain would come on and say we had another weight situation, and the groundskeepers needed to take care of it. Rather than waiting I would hop off the plane and go back to the same mess I was in. Once I got off that plane, it took right off, and I was left shaking my head and making excuses. But if I had just packed the necessary things, I could have moved on too.

Each relationship has its own weight requirements. Some relationships can handle a considerable amount of weight while others can't. This does not mean you and this person aren't meant to be. Actually it means you are not packed appropriately.

Every trip we take requires the common necessities, like your toiletries, underwear, and certain clothes depending on the season. After that the other items depend on what you plan on doing on the trip. If you are going to the beach, I surely hope you didn't pack a North Face down jacket with a pair of ski pants and some Sarah Palin boots. Yes, I did say Sarah Palin boots. I hope you packed you a really cute swimsuit or some really nice trunks. That is the problem for a lot of us, though. We are wandering around wearing rain suits while there is not a cloud in the sky. Everyone around you wants to know why you've got that wretched thing on. And there you are, reminiscing about a day way back when, when the wind blew the clouds in, and your favorite outfit got drenched, and your perm was rained out. Fellas, don't grin too hard. I am going to take a walk down your street too. Some of you are still remembering when your fresh pair of Jordans got destroyed. Now, if there is one thing I have learned about Jays through the years, it is this: if you have some sort of sense, you don't wear them out in the rain. This is why how you pack is very vital to your situation.

How do I properly pack? I think that out of everything, this is one of the most essential questions we all must ask ourselves before we even make that trip. See, we have already found our destinations, and we have bought our tickets. Now it is up to us to check out the Weather Channel or look online at the various weather reports and choose our wardrobes accordingly. Depending on the area you are traveling to, you know the possibilities for climate and weather changes. I know if anyone travels to Louisville, Kentucky, for the derby, they should pack some nice linen as well as some shorts, polos, and sandals. During the Kentucky Derby, various celebrities come into town and put on events here and there, so if you want to go, pack accordingly. You will find the usual dress-to-impress, black-tie affairs and club functions. Please make sure you are prepared, and bring an umbrella. There's always a slight chance of rain. If you don't plan accordingly, you may very well get caught in a terrential downpour with no protection.That's right—you're thinking, *Man, if I had just done this or that...*Life does not revolve around what you should have done, could have done, or would have done, so please pack wisely.

I hope after reading this chapter, you will understand that no, these bags are not free. Many of us have the presumption that the best things in life are free, and what one doesn't know can't hurt them. Everything in our life costs something. There isn't one thing under the sun that doesn't require our attention, our time, our efforts, or our hearts. We can't continue under the assumption that ignorance is bliss.

No, you will never see an additional charge at the airport because of your emotional baggage, but I am sure your vacation would be better if you just released those bags. Many of you are on the brink of a breakthrough if you would just finally decide to let your guard down. I know it is hard, but once you quit hoarding and harboring those ill feelings, the negative emotions that happened yesterday, you can have life anew today. History is not to be dwelled on, but we are meant to learn from it. Yes, what he or she did hurt you, but that doesn't mean the next person is going to hurt you. That is the point of this chapter.

All hell might have broken loose in your life, but you somehow didn't break. They say what doesn't kill you makes you stronger, and it is true. Quit wasting your life focusing on the rearview. It is hard to avoid obstacles if you can't see them coming at you. Many of you are in positions to fly, but you are weighed down too much to take off. All I ask is that you pack wisely and be sure to bring only the necessities when you are flying Romantic Airlines to the Rest of Our Lives Resort.

Like · Comment · Share

4

Almost Had You

Richard Rowland Jr.

Why does it seem so hard to say good-bye to yesterday? Men and women seem to be carrying emotional baggage because it is so hard to find closure after a break up. Most people just disappear without a trace or muttering and mumbling when things go wrong. Is this a good or bad thing? How does one get back on his or her feet after feeling this horrid pain?

Like · Comment · Share

Comments

Tara Richard, this is not good at all. If it is at all possible, people should at least try to part as friends, to say the least. Knowing what I know now, I believe it is important for people to have closure to their relationships. If you don't it could very well lead to an awkward experience. Have you ever run into your ex while out on the town? Awkward, right? Imagine if you didn't get closure. Getting back on your feet is a very difficult thing to do, and it is easier said than done. Regardless of that fact, you have to keep going on in hopes that things won't be the same the next go around.

Troy After a breakup, I believe, it is important that everyone receives some type of closure. I believe it allows individuals to learn about issues that weren't brought to the table during the relationship. People tend to overlook issues and bottle up emotions throughout their relationships because they are afraid to face problems.

In my life it is important for me to reach closure because I feel like it helps me for my future relationships. It teaches me about the shortcomings I never even knew I had, and it prepares me for my next partner. Sometimes it takes someone to point out the obvious to me in order for me to make the necessary corrections to me as a person.

Like · Comment · Share

Richard Rowland Jr.

I believe that most people want to seek closure in relationships, but getting there can be difficult. Sometimes the relationship has taken so much out of you that you don't even want to be bothered with it anymore. Let's think about our past relationships for a little bit. I can't speak for anyone but myself. I was fortunate to have women in my life who I felt were worth seeking closure from. We may not have seen eye to eye, but we believed that ending our relationships on some form of a high note was important.

I find that communication is key to both moving on and maintaining a healthy relationship. Closure can be the key to someone moving on to the next relationship without the heavy bags and luggage of their last breakup. I feel, though, in some ways closure is like an exit interview at a job that you just couldn't stand anymore. If you have already put in your two weeks' notice or letter of resignation, why do you still need to meet with your soon to be ex-boss to talk about it?

I fully understand that I have written two paragraphs that contradict themselves, and I did that because I am fifty/fifty on the closure idea. Yes, closure is good in some cases. I believe that sometimes closure doesn't have to come from a deep conversation with a soon to be or already ex. Maybe we just need to take a look in the mirror and reflect on how the relationship was. Did we do all we could do to make it work? Were we the best we could be? Did we take the person for granted? Did we underappreciate him or her?

Also flip it on the other person. Do we feel he or she did all those for us? In the end we will be able to find closure that way as well.

As many of my friends know about me, I don't like wasting my breath or time on things. Sometimes it is written on the wall, and, ladies and gentlemen, it is what it is.

Like · Comment · Share

Nia Richard, I hope you don't mind me piggybacking off of your job analogy. I believe when anyone gives two weeks' notice, he or she is showing his or her former employer that he or she does care. In this situation the former employer has ample time to find someone to fill the empty position.

Jennifer K Richard, I completely agree with this notion that closure is a great tool for helping people let go of their emotional baggage. I think people need first to forgive themselves as well as the other person they were involved with. I understand this is a hard thing to do in some cases, but it is very necessary in order for anyone to move on.

Like · Comment · Share

Richard Rowland Jr.

Jennifer, how do we deal with the issue if it is our partner who is having a hard time letting go of these pent-up emotions? How do we get him or her to release this heartache and pain?

Jennifer K Wow, Richard. I can't believe you put me on the spot like that. I am just playing, by the way. I guess the easy answer is to stick it out, but that can be a tough thing to do. Love can take only so much. I know in the past, I have dealt with things in a relationship just because I loved him, but that got old quickly. After a while I would confront my significant other about his emotional baggage, and I brought how bad it made me feel to his attention. From that moment on, he was ready to go through the process of improvement. He was game for professional, church, or any sort of counseling. That is the same thing we all have to be ready to do, and if those things don't work you have to be prepared to dissolve the relationship. There comes a point in time when you have to face the hurt head on and stop carrying it with you to other relationships. It can't be your excuse to keep your partner and the new relationship at a standstill because of yesterday's news.

Charles You can't help someone break from something or someone he or she chooses to hold on to. That's a heart matter. It is one thing for someone to have a hurtful past experience or relationship, but the question is, is he or she wholeheartedly committed to allowing a new relationship to grow? A fun and new relationship can be just what the doctor ordered. I am not saying hop into and out of relationships to fill your emotional vacancies. The problem lies in when we allow our pasts to be barriers preventing the healing process, and we must understand the healing process is letting go of what is holding us down. I hope this isn't a sexist statement (that's not my intent), but many women need closure when it comes to reconciling what went wrong in a relationship. Closure is critical to healing. The best guidance in this case is to follow the three Ps—be prayerful, be patient, be present—and receive your blessings.

Ernest Everyone carries baggage into his or her relationships, whether it comes from a past relationship, a family issue, or a personal issue. The key is whether or not you allow your baggage to mess up a relationship that can blossom into something great. Hopefully the person you are in the new relationship with is enriching you to the point that you realize the baggage you brought in is not a reflection of who you are and how your new relationship has to be. The best way to combat baggage is communication between two serious adults in a loving relationship. If those factors are absent then throw in the towel and move on.

Wanda Prayer helps, and knowing that in time wounds heal should be a soothing fact. The thing about emotional scars is you can see them as scars and hang on to them or you can see them as lessons learned and move on stronger than ever. We can't control what happens to us, but we can control our reactions to what happens.

Nakia When I was younger, my grandfather taught me an incredible equation. He said that forgiveness of self and others plus time equals a healed heart and a healed soul.

Jaime Richard, my personal take on this is that one can only hope he or she is not the rebound. We all carry some form of baggage, and even if we desperately want not to bring it into our current relationships, sometimes it creeps in. This can occur when we look through photo albums, hear an old song, and the list goes on and on. It also depends on the circumstances behind the baggage, meaning was it cheating (on either's part), who ended the relationship, and why did the relationship end? It's important that the individual realizes baggage is just another form of lessons learned. Life is all about lessons, and we all view things differently while learning at different speeds. Have patience with yourself and your significant other. If things are meant to be, they will be.

Jennifer K Love it, Jaime! If it's meant to be, it will be!

Like · Comment · Share

Richard Rowland Jr.

People always say, "If it's meant to be, it will be." My question to these individuals is, "Will it be?" And if the answer is it will, please tell me, how shall it come to pass? Nothing is ever meant to be or set in stone. A valuable point I have learned in my life is men and women have the God-given right to choose their actions and behaviors, which have consequences and repercussions that are not predetermined. The only thing that is predestined in our lives is that we will live and then die. In the words of Drizzy "Drake" Rogers, from the song "Moments for Life," "everybody dies, but not everybody lives."

Let's revisit this phrase "if it's meant to be, it will be" and drill down a little deeper. Karyn Ravn, author of *Our Inward Journey*, believes "only as high as I reach can I grow, only as far as I seek can I go; only as deep as I look can I see, only as much as I dream can I be." The phrase in question begins with the conjunction *if*. The word, ladies and gentlemen, is not only a conjunction but, more specifically, a subordinating conjunction. What is the big deal about this profound fact? For all of you who aren't English scholars, a conjunction precedes a clause that is dependent on the rest of the sentence. After reading this wouldn't you agree that the statement "if it's meant to be, it will be" requires whatever "it" is to do some work to help make it happen?

In the world of computers, programmers have learned how to embrace the power of the word *if*. Not to get too technical, programmers have the ability to tell a program to do something, but it requires an action. For instance, if you click "start" on a particular program, it will start, or else it won't. The program's starting up is dependent on your pressing the "start" button. Does that make sense?

How does that work in your life? Well, if you and someone work hard at a relationship, it may work, but there are always a variety of variables that can play their parts in this. Unlike computer programs we cannot make this an absolute. Why can't we? Because unlike programs we don't have to obey certain commands. Remember we have the gift of free will. Many of you have been in relationships with the loves of your lives, but things didn't quite work out. I can attest to that myself. The problem was neither of us was mature enough to make it work. I am sure the same can be said for some of your relationships.

I am begging you, please stop going through this life looking for someone who is meant to be with you. The problem with the phrase is it underwrites the importance of past events and your ability to deal with them. In the last chapter, we posed the question, "Do bags fly for free?" I know by now all of you would say, "No, they do not." Emotional baggage is the reason why things aren't meant to be. The choices we make are the reasons why relationships aren't meant to be. The things we value are the reasons why you and the love of your life can't experience a great relationship. Believe me, I know it's hard out there, but please don't make it even harder on yourself by living a lie. I am sure all of you have heard the phrase "the truth hurts," but I would argue that lies hurt even more. Stop lying to yourself, and stop lying to your friends. There is nothing beneath this sun that is meant to be except life and death. The rest is up to you. I hate to say this corny line, but it is so true: knowing is truly only half the battle.

I know it's hard to accept change, but in order to carry on, you have to. Many of you out there hate change and don't want anything different. Earlier I said the only two things you can expect in life are living and dying. I may have spoken too soon. Change is something else we can expect in our lives. Every day we are growing a little older and, hopefully, a little wiser. Every day we grow closer to another season's change. Stop fighting it, and just learn to embrace it.

One reason why a number of you are sitting there all alone is you didn't understand that relationships change, love changes, and people change over time. You might find this surprising, but yes, even you change, in some cases for the better and in other cases for the worst. That is the very reason why each and every day, we must make the decision to fight for our love or not. The person you fall in love with today will not be the same person twenty years down the road. The person you are dating right now will not be that man or woman when you marry him or her. The person you are interested in will be a different person tomorrow. Human beings are things of circumstance, and who we are is affected by the ifs and what ifs. Some of you are making relationship decisions based on the ifs. I will marry so and so if this happens. If you do this for me, I will do this for you. This maybe a hard pill to swallow, but it is the truth.

The question we need to focus on is: why does it seem so hard to say good-bye to yesterday? Why do we all seem to get stuck in the so-called good ole days? Were they truly the good ole days? If so, why didn't you stay there in the first place?

A lot of us seem to be stuck on the things we used to do, the places we used to go, and the people we used to be around. From time to time, even I have something that sets off wonderful memories of yesterday. I have a tub of keep-sakes in which I have all the letters I received from every woman who showed interest in me. I have letters from and pictures of ex-girlfriends and women I met over the Internet from all over the world, and I have special reminders of my younger days. Opening up this box sends me down memory lane, and I must admit I have some great memories. I grew up with an incredible family that loved me, and my childhood experience was one I dare anyone to try to compete with. Life wasn't perfect, but you couldn't tell me that way back then. I grew up with a great group of friends. When I moved to Louisville after my parents divorced, I met a cool group of people in the city that I keep in touch with to this day. While all of these are such grand things, I can't go back to those days. Normally when we reflect, we think of the good things. Then there are others who look back over their lives and see only the bad.

It is so hard to say good-bye to yesterday because we won't do it. I know this is easier said than done, but sooner or later you just have to let it go. So what if things didn't turn out like you wanted them to? Keep on keeping on. A lot of you see the pain in a breakup, see the difficulty in change, but ladies and gentleman, we have to understand that when we experience setbacks in our lives, they are opportunities for God to set us up for comebacks. You and ole girl broke up because you guys weren't meant to be. You and ole boy broke up because you had no business being with him in the first place. I am a firm believer that regardless of what is going on in my life, God has something far better for me than I can ever begin to fathom. You will never be able to experience this blessing if you are still stuck on a mess from way back when.

I understand that human nature says there is a reason why everything happens. Stop lying to yourself. Things in life happen because they happen. Stop attributing everything to outside forces. This isn't rocket science. I admit it would be great if you guys could sit down and have one last powwow and then go your separate ways, but it's not going to always happen like that. If your significant other did happen to leave for a reason, you probably know what it is. Were you taking care of your responsibilities, or were you neglecting them? Did you feel the division between the two of you, or were you oblivious to something everyone else already knew?

Ladies and gentlemen, relationships don't just happen. They require hard work. Both individuals must first be in tune with themselves, then they must pay close attention to detail and be in tune with one another. Oftentimes couples go into relationships believing that love will see them through anything the future may bring. Who knows what tomorrow may hold? The moral of the story is this: we each have to look at our relationships not as they are but as they can be. A mature person always visualizes what can be done in the future. He or she isn't stuck in the present. Why is this important? Because it is much easier to fall in love than to stay in love. The problem is from time to time couples let their guards down and take each other for granted. We each have to do our best not to get complacent or too comfortable. Furthermore we must be in tune with our significant others to ensure the relationships do work.

A great example of this took place in *Why Did I Get Married Too?* In the film Tyler Perry's character, Terry Brock, witnesses a change in his wife—Sharon Leal's character, Dianne Brock. She strangely modifies her routine. Every morning Terry watches how Dianne now meticulously selects her wardrobe for work. She even spends a considerable amount of time searching for sexy brassieres and underwear to wear. He also notices that after work, she is always in a seductive mood. I am quite sure this sounds innocent, but in the first movie, *Why Did I Get Married?*, Terry couldn't get any intimate attention from his wife because she focused more on her career than on her husband.

Mr. and Mrs. Brock's marriage almost ended in divorce because of Dianne's neglecting her husband. Now in the second film, Dianne is spending time worrying about her appearance when she leaves the house. Funny thing is the story will change.

I understand it is very important for women to feel sexy, but Dianne's escapade sticks out. While she does her best to look sexy when she walks out the door to go to work, she doesn't do the same when she gets home. When she comes home to her husband, she puts on the most unappealing pajamas to sleep in. It shouldn't be a surprise that this didn't sit well with me. I was thinking, *Woman, what are you doing when you go to work?*

Finally Terry decides that enough is enough. One day he does the unthinkable when Mrs. Brock comes home from work in one of her seductive moods. This time he can't hold back any longer. He confronts his wife. He explains how he has noticed how she has changed over the last couple of months. During the exchange he says something powerful that stood out to me: "Honey, I love your heartbeat. I know it. I am in tune with you. You can't be this arrogant. You can't think I wasn't paying attention."

What would have happened if that were you? Would you have noticed that your mate changed his or her routine? I would like to play devil's advocate and say yes, but I already know most of us aren't that in tune with ourselves let alone our mates. That is why things just happen. In the movie the conversation concluded with Dianne stating, "I am asking you these things because I am trying to save this marriage, trying to save us." Are you willing to stay in tune with your significant other to save your relationship?

Some of you have missed out on life because you are still stuck on yesterday. You are still baffled by the fact that so and so left without giving you a reason. Some of you knew the reason a long time ago, but you are shocked that he or she ever had the audacity to leave. I am well aware that closure helps you become better as a partner, but I also believe reflection does as well.

Sit back and do a little unbiased introspection. Surely you can muster up memories of your relationship. Some of you can't say good-bye to yesterday because you know you didn't put your all into the relationship. Now you sit there wanting to blame so and so for your emotional baggage, but every single time you point your finger at him or her, I hope you notice those three other fingers pointing back at you, reminding you that you dropped the ball on some occasions.

In some situations it may take someone else to point out where you failed, but for the most post part you already know. Whenever I think of the beautiful relationships I had, there isn't a time that I don't go, "Man, I really messed up when I did this," or, "I really made a bonehead decision when I did that." We can't get stuck on the shoulda, coulda, wouldas of life. The world is changing each and every day, and we have to follow suit. I don't care how you do it, but realize that the longer you focus on mistakes, the longer it will take you to get back on your feet.

While working on this project, I had the opportunity and pleasure of meeting a human being who is very beautiful inside and out. Her name is Ms. Bonnie St. John, and she is the author of numerous books. She is a winter Paralympic medalist, and she was a Rhodes Scholar, just to name a couple of her accomplishments. This wonderful woman was giving a speech about her life during an Urban League event in Louisville, and she said some profound words I want to share with you. She said that regardless of the way things go in your life, it is up to you to get back up. She said life will set some obstacles in your path, but you have to muster the strength to try to maneuver around them or jump over them, and if you trip you've got to get back up.

This woman was the first African American to earn a medal in the winter Paralympics. During her record-setting ski race, she had a pretty smooth ride down the beautiful mountain slopes, and all seemed to be going well. She was headed for the gold, and no one was going to catch her. She was skiing toward history. She and her opponent were neck and neck, and it looked like this would be a photo finish when all of a sudden, both skiers took falls for an unforeseen reason. They were lengths ahead of the pack, and they somehow stumbled. Bonnie lay in the snow, hurt and dejected. She did her best to get up. Sadly the other skier got up faster than she did and got a gold medal while Bonnie won a silver medal.

The lesson she learned from that experience is that life is not always about success. Life is about taking on a challenge and conquering it. You may be missing out on your success because you waited too long to get up. Stop wasting time and get up. If Bonnie had gotten up sooner than her opponent, she would have been a gold medalist. That is definitely how life is. There isn't a divine plan that you and a particular individual are going to get together, so I suggest you get off your butt, put down the tub of ice cream, and go out and love again.

I believe that a number of you have had your Mr. or Mrs. Right come into your life and then suddenly ride off into the sunset without mumbling a single word, leaving you hurt, distraught, and in some cases emotionally dead. Maybe you have never had someone walk out on you like that, but you have been the individual who just exited stage left for no apparent reason. If you did someone like this, please don't get all bent out of shape because I have been exactly where you have been, and I now sit here from time to time wondering, *What if I had just given our love a chance?* My deepest regret is that I was such a coward, I didn't break up with her in person or on the phone. I dropped this horrible bombshell on the woman I claimed to love on the Internet, via e-mail. Ouch!

Looking back at this decision, I admit it wasn't a very good idea. I owed her more respect than that. I can still remember the day she called me after reading the e-mail. I was in my dorm room with my Zach Morris phone. For those of you who aren't familiar with a Zach Morris phone, they were those huge Nokias that could get rolled over by a tank and wouldn't break or crack for anything. Sadly I was on a one-sided phone call as one of the most beautiful women I had met in my life cried her heart out to me. This is the part that hurts me more than anything. I agree with my decision to this day. I believe we needed to break up because I wasn't mature enough to handle the relationship. I just don't believe I ended it in the most appropriate way to. Beautiful, if you are reading these words, I am so sorry for what I did to you then. I am so happy you allowed me to be your friend after your wounds healed. Congrats on you and your husband's first baby.

Why did I leave this woman in such a coldhearted manner? Looking back on it, I believe I just found myself in a situation similar to Chris Brown's when he wrote the song "Say Goodbye." I was sitting and waiting for the most perfect and opportune time to tell my lovely girlfriend that I believed we should go our separate ways, and in the end I waited till I was backed into a corner, and I hurt her horribly.

The major problems this lovely lady and I had were attributable to our not communicating. The sad part is she was communicating while I was not. I know with my heart that if I had opened up to her and told her I thought she was being too clingy, things would have had the possibility to get better. Maybe if I had told her she shouldn't focus so much on getting married and just take time to enjoy our relationship, everything would have been OK. Notice I used the word *if* in these statements. If I had spoken up, and if she had granted my wishes, we would have been meant to be.

At this very instant, many of you may want to take your relationships to the next level despite the issues that come at you. There are also a number of you who have found yourselves in losing battles, and you just don't know what to do. You are ready to say good-bye, but you don't know how to begin.

I believe that a deeper analysis of Chris Brown's song will aid you in your decision. In "Say Goodbye" he explains that "there's never a right time to say good-bye," but you have to make the first move sooner rather than later. He further explains that you must make this move because if you don't, the one you love the most will end up hating you, and you really don't want to burn that bridge. I hope none of you will make the same mistake I did. I was blessed to have an incredible girlfriend who loved me enough to look past my boneheaded decision, and we were able to foster a stronger friendship than we had even while we were dating.

If you all haven't figured it out by now, I will just spell it out for you. Why did I make this boneheaded move? Because as a younger man, I didn't know how to deal with a woman's shedding tears or being emotional. I could never find the right words to say good-bye. I knew whatever words I said would hurt her so much that she would be brought to tears, or at least I assumed she would. The saddest part is I didn't want to deal with my own emotions. I knew that no matter how I explained it to her, our relationship wasn't going to work. I felt she was going to become quite emotional because that was her. Sending her an impersonal e-mail meant I wasn't going to have to deal with it personally. I felt she would be so enraged by the e-mail, she wouldn't even want to hear my voice again. I was wrong.

Many of you have sat yourselves out of the dating game for too long, and it is time to come back onto the field of play. I realize that breaking up with someone is really hard. But if you love him or her, you will do it the right way—you will be civil, and you will do your best to give him or her closure. For all of you saying, "Well, so and so didn't give me closure," you can stop making that excuse now and move on. If someone has the audacity of just riding off into the sunset of your life, he or she is a coward, and you should keep on keeping on. Somewhere down the road, you'll have to be woman or man enough to say good-bye to the thing you love the most, which is the memory of yesterday, when everything seemed to be going so well.

Boyz II Men teaches us a very valuable lesson in their song "It's So Hard to Say Goodbye to Yesterday." While listening to this wonderful song, I learned that even in our deepest and darkest hours, we should somehow be man or woman enough to take with us the memories of yesterday to be our sunshine after the rain, even though it will truly be hard to say good-bye to yesterday. Not every relationship is promised success, and sometimes you have to walk away no matter how hard it may seem. We have to recognize that yes, this is indeed a setback that can be a setup for God to give us an incredible comeback.

I would like to think that by now each of you realizes the importance of closure. I also know I can sit here and assume all day, but that doesn't mean all of you are grasping how critical closure can be to both men and women. Some of you might be asking the question, "Why is closure so impactful on individuals' future emotional endeavors?" Well, you need to understand that all of us need to find the ability to turn the page. Sometimes in our lives, we need assistance moving on to the next chapter, and I hope that at this very moment I am providing that nudge in the right direction. I don't want you all to go through what I had to go through.

Unfortunately this closure thing bit me right in the patootie. I was dating a very beautiful young lady in college who just so happened to have closure issues. In her life she'd had the ill fortune of having a boyfriend who vanished for three years. He actually hadn't vanished; he had graduated from high school and gone into the navy. Their communication died off during his basic training, but that is something I learned later on down the road.

I was in the second semester of my sophomore year of college when I met this young lady from Tennessee. The relationship was nowhere near a walk in the park for us because we didn't have the slightest clue about healthy communication. I won't sit here and act like we didn't try to talk, but the problem was the communication would completely shut down. For some odd reason, she wouldn't let her hair down and just be open with me. She was far more open with me than with anyone else, but still she still wasn't open enough, and that bothered me. We would have deep, meaningful conversations, but I always got the feeling she was showing me only the tip of the iceberg. It always felt like she was telling me enough just to get by, and her eyes always seemed to show me that she had much more on her mind even though she would claim she didn't.

Our relationship ended because she cheated on me with her high school sweetheart. I believe if she and I had had deep, meaningful conversations, we wouldn't have gone down that path. I am not saying if you don't have meaningful conversations with your significant other, he or she is going to cheat on you, but I am saying you will be well aware of where he or she is coming from if both of you are honest. If she had let me know that she still deeply loved this man she hadn't been in a relationship with for so many years, I never would have gotten in a relationship with her to begin with. I would have just remained a good friend, and I wouldn't have had to deal with being cheated on. I wouldn't have had to deal with having to break up with someone I had been in a relationship with for two and a half years. After we broke up, I had to put all the pieces of my life back together. I thank God I was able to do it in a short amount of time.

Many of you out there have had horrible breakups, and you are probably wondering how I was ever able to get back up at all. Earlier I posed this question: how does one get back on his or her feet after suffering defeat at the hands of a failed relationship? Before I answer this question, I want you to understand there isn't a be all, end all answer. There isn't one absolute truth. First and foremost, you as an individual must make the decision to drop these bags. Many of you are hoping for someone to walk into your lives and take the bags from you, but they can't. Matters of the heart weigh heavy on a person, and the only way to get rid of this unneeded burden is to commit yourself fully to removing it from your life. Emotional baggage can be a cancer that ruins your outlook on life. Unfortunately there isn't any chemotherapy or any medicine to remove it. This is a matter of the heart, and your only help is God. It is up to you to work diligently to find ways of removing it. Let that marinate for a second.

You are sitting here waiting on the first step to removing emotional baggage from your life, and we already said that the first step is deciding to get rid of it. However, if you are a very stubborn individual, the only way something is going to happen is if your hardheaded self decides you will do it. You can pray three hundred and sixty-five days a year, and you can anoint your body with oils and holy water every day, and nothing will happen till your attitude changes. We are in the places where we are because of our thinking processes. Our viewpoints are critical to everything we do, so please take the first step. Agree you aren't going to deal with these heavy bags anymore, and step out on faith. No, you may not know where you are going next, but you know it won't be with this heavy burden on your heart, and that is good enough. Just believe that where you are going and who you will meet will be better than it was before.

Many of you are missing out on beautiful relationships because you want them to be like the one you had before. I know that is why I missed out on a number of great relationships—because I waited on the ex-girlfriend who broke up with me two days before I graduated from college to give me another chance. The saddest part of this story is that it's now five years later, and we still haven't tried again. She actually just broke up with her boyfriend, and we have hung out a couple times, but things have changed, and we are far better friends than we ever could be lovers.

In the book *ReCreating Your Self: Making the Changes that Set You Free*, Neale Donald Walsch explains that "pain is a result of your failure to see and understand that perspective creates reality." According to Walsch, "reality is always changing and that means that our perspective is always changing. The pain many of us feel comes from our desperate search for anything that doesn't change and remains the way it is found." Here we are, shedding tears and missing out on life because we are still allowing the feelings of yesterday to affect us today. We are missing out on turning the pages of life because we are focusing on what we missed out on rather than on what we can gain in the future.

For those of you who are hurting like I am, I suggest you stop fighting the process and allow yourself to go with the flow. The more you try to fight against the change you can't stop, the more you will end up submerged in a pool of your own tears. Whether you want to believe it or not, change will have its way, and you will have to deal with it. I suggest you make up your mind and let go of the emotional baggage that is holding you down. There will come a day when you have to decide your exit strategy. In the process be prayerful, patient, and present for when your blessings come. I said be prayerful, be patient, and be present for when your blessings do come in.

In the end I would like to leave you all with a public service announcement. Sooner or later you will have to let go of your baggage if you want to be set free from your emotional captivity. Your quality of life will improve once you let go and let God. Stop missing your blessings because you are still stuck on him or her. Yesterday died last night at midnight, so enjoy the present, and look forward to the mystery of the future. Some of you are probably still going to remain stubborn and harbor old feelings for whatever reason. You are in luck. I did my work, and I have prepared something especially for you.

At this very moment, you could be missing out on the best thing that ever happened to your life, but you are too blind to notice him or her. Why are you too blind? I don't know. Why don't you tell me the reason? I am sure you know exactly why. I believe that many of you are suffering from the same problem I was. Many of you are still stuck on yesterday. You may have had the strength to move on and find someone new, but you still lack the strength to get over the hump. There you are, looking at old photo albums, listening to your and your boo's favorite song, and still cooking his or her favorite meal even though he or she is never coming home to eat it. You even had the audacity to ask this new special someone to wear some smell goods your ex used to wear, but you didn't tell your newfound love that. You just told him or her it smells good. You are going out to restaurants that remind you of your ex; you are renting movies you all used to watch; and from time to time you almost call your new friend your ex's name, and that is not a good look whatsoever. Since you clearly got it bad for you know who, I believe it is only right for me to help you out.

Tamia, in her song "Almost," speaks of how you can miss out on the love of your life if you don't just let go and give love a chance. There you are, sitting in front of one of the most beautiful or most handsome people you could ever come across, and guess what? You are too afraid to let go of something that has been long gone. Despite your fears this wonderful person has taken the time to grow an interest in you. Little do you know that behind closed doors, this wonderful individual is shedding tears and feeling alone because he or she just doesn't understand why you aren't giving him or her a chance. He or she is being patient. He or she isn't rushing you, and you still find a way to play this person to the left emotionally. In his or her heart, he or she believes you are right for him or her. Even though you know in your heart that this person is right for you, you still wait on yesterday to reappear.

I hate to be the bearer of bad news, but yesterday is gone. The present is here, and you need to understand that tomorrow is up in the air. Right now you are in the best position to be in. You have great things brewing in your life. You have the potential of committing to the best thing that ever happened to you, but you aren't sure if it's meant to be or not. We all have to make the decision if a particular love is worth fighting for and then fight for it. Don't talk the talk; walk the walk. I'm begging you please to stop wasting time and learn to live and love now. I understand it is easier said than done, but you will never learn anything if you don't get out there and try.

At this very moment, I know, all of you stubborn individuals are like, "Man, everything is fine. You don't know what I went through, and you don't know me from Adam or Eve."

True, I don't know your struggle, and I don't know you, but I do know how it feels to love someone deeply and to miss out on love, and believe me, I definitely have felt some pain. I just want you to let go, let God, and love because I don't want you to follow my self-destructive path. Here I am, a seasoned young man of thirty-plus years, writing you about love because I was too stubborn to let go and live in the now rather than marinating in the past.

When I sat down and listened to Pandora.com on my iPod, I was introduced to the beautiful melody of Tamia's song. In it she sings some profound questions I want to ask you. She sings:

Can you tell me
How can one miss what she's never had?
How could I reminisce when there is no past?
How could I have memories of being happy with you, boy?
Could someone tell me how can this be?
How could my mind pull up incidents,
Recall dates and times that never happened?
How could we celebrate a love that's too late?

These words gave me the strength to step out of the emotional prison in which I had placed myself. I was focusing on yesterday, and that day had come and gone. I was free to do as I pleased, but I was still stuck on old news. I was holding the key to my freedom; I just wasn't mustering the strength to get up and unlock the door.

How could Tamia reminisce about all of those things she never had? She could do that because your viewpoint is critical. She could do that because your perspective creates your reality. I believe if Tamia had just made the decision to let go of the past, she would have been just fine, but because she held on, all she could have were shoulda, coulda, woulda memories that she called "almost moments." That's where a lot of you are. That's where I was when I began this Facebook memoir movement. By the grace of God, I have been loosed from my chains, and I am emotionally ready to love again.

I know the scars from a break up are hard to heal from, but you have to understand not everyone comes into your life to be there forever. Some come but for a brief season, and you have to be mature enough to let them go. You have to know that God uses setbacks as ways to set you up for comebacks.

Don't cry anymore. Don't hold on to your past anymore. Please leave it. Learn to love and learn to live again. I know it will be hard at first, but I assure you that you will find love, and you will live life more abundantly. Emotional baggage shouldn't be a hindrance. The memories of yesterday shouldn't hold you back; they should prepare you for the days to come. These painful situations are here to help us move on to be stronger, wiser, and brighter people.

Like · Comment · Share

5

Looking for Love in All the Wrong Places

Richard Rowland Jr.

We have discussed how each and every one of us has some degree of emotional baggage. We have even considered the fact that bags do not fly for free. We have contemplated which bags are necessary and which are unnecessary for our journeys. Still a question persists: even when all the bags seem to be checked in, why does all hell break loose in our lives? Why do our relationships still not work the way we want them to?

Like · Comment · Share

Richard Rowland Jr.

The key reason relationships are failing is we are settling for status when we should be seeking potential, and that means a deeper look beyond an individual's physical beauty and bank statements.

Shelley I think it's selfishness and self-centered thinking. Being in a relationship requires two individuals to love wholeheartedly. Even loving the other person more than you love yourself and wanting that person to be happy. This only works if the feelings are reciprocated. When each person loves the other, gives of himself or herself, and wants what's best for the other then as a single person you become stronger. In turn this makes you unbreakable. All issues you hear about, especially infidelity, stem from selfishness in one or both partners.

Brandon I think it is the fact that people fall for the belief that relationships are supposed to be perfect or not at all. A real relationship and even a marriage has its trials and tribulations. It is the resilience of that relationship that determines whether or not it is destined for success or failure. We all have our hang-ups and idiosyncrasies, but as long as you love the person you are with all else is up to an open line of communication and trying to understand your partner.

Jennifer Real talk, there are so many reasons why many relationships nowadays don't work. Statistics show societal and economic factors lead to an imbalance in mate selection (i.e., women outnumber men in educational aspects, which leads to incompatibility). Everyone wants someone he or she is compatible with. Society believes those who attend college are more cultured, mature, and stable and think in terms of long-term goals. Some believe if you take this equation into account, an educated individual plus an uneducated person equals a relationship failure.

Personally I believe society has become lazy and self-centered (as Shelley mentioned), relies on convenience, and lacks a spiritual foundation. People run around like consumers, picking out lovers based on what is good to them. When things don't work out, they hastily run to the next person instead of working toward a meaningful relationship. Our ancestors came up in an era where sticking it out through thick and thin was the norm. This meant they were willing to battle to withstand any type of struggle that came their way. Today, after one little argument, a mate is ready to call it quits.

A lazy mentality is quite evident. Not to mention society has become entirely too self-centered. People are walking through life thinking only about themselves. For instance, the sort of requirements people expect from their mates: I want Mr. or Mrs. Right now…He must earn… She has to have a big…Any of those sound familiar? In my opinion this stems from the persuasive messages found in music and media. People

are consumed by personal gratification even though we all know relationships aren't about just one person. At least they aren't meant to
be. When a person truly wants to be in a relationship, he or she doesn't
think in singular terms; rather he or she has a "we" mind-set where an
equal portion of compromise and sacrifice dwells.

Shenika Jennifer, you better preach, girl. I agree with you wholeheartedly. I have encountered so many women who want to be able to say,
"I have a man," and they don't know themselves yet. This is something
I struggled with myself. Ladies, we have to stop settling for anything
and make sure we connect with brothers on our level. I am sick and
tired of seeing sisters who are doing big things in their own right dating
guys who have no future. It would be one thing if they were trying, but
these guys don't care about their futures. They are just sitting at home,
mooching off you. If you are an independent woman, why are you with
a man who sells drugs, lives with Momma, and doesn't have any goals?

George I believe it is insecurity.

Johnnie Communication and a lack of trust.

Troy Here are my two cents. People are constructively dissatisfied with
themselves as well as their partners, which leads them to search for the
next best thing. Nobody's perfect; you just have to figure out the qualities
you would like your partner to possess and learn to deal with the rest. Plus,
I believe, some relationships fall apart because of quality time. My relationship fell apart because my girl and I worked different shifts. Opposite
shifts tend to put a bind on the relationship. It is always good to get some
time away from your significant other, but too much time is dangerous.
It's hard to get by when you see each other only on the weekends.

Tara The reason relationships are failing is people aren't putting God
into them. Relationships aren't working because couples are not

building them on the solid rock. God needs to be involved in our marriages and relationships. We need to learn to consult with the Father because we need to know if this relationship is in his will. We need to task him for understanding so we can know if this individual should even be in our life. I believe having a holy consultation is the answer to all the problems in our lives. God should be included in all aspects of our lives.

Shenika I saw you at church this morning, Richard, so I know that you already heard the powerful message Pastor Dr. Jasmine Scurlok brought us from York, Pennsylvania, on Women's Weekend. I agree wholeheartedly with Tara, and I believe that we must trust God first and then watch everything fall in line according to his will. In relationships many of us, including me, lose sight of pleasing God and focus on pleasing him or her, and this is the reason why our relationships fall apart. You may not be selfish, but you just so happen to be in a relationship with someone who is, and now you are forced to love him or her more than you love yourself, and that is not a good situation. Maybe you are selfish, and now you are forcing your significant other to love you more than he or she loves himself or herself. A family, couple, marriage, union, or whatever you want to call it that prays together stays together because the common goal is for each of you in that union to please God and not yourself.

Jessica Relationships are hard. You have to work at them, and this isn't meant to be a solo feat. Both of you have to work hard at it. Things don't just happen to fall into place. Loving someone means you are agreeing to love them for his or her faults and baggage because that is essentially who he or she is. Some baggage gets lost along the way, but somehow, in some way, these bags can find their way back.

Self-awareness allows you to see the true you and helps you understand who you want to be versus who you are. The same goes for your partner.

If he or she doesn't love himself or herself, he or she can't possibly love you. You have to learn to accept your baggage as a part of you. In the end you might notice that the baggage wasn't as much as you thought it was. Until you can accept it, you can't accept your significant other's faults because you are too busy looking for things to fill your imperfect void.

Like · Comment · Share

Richard Rowland Jr.

Why are our relationships falling apart? Couples are splitting up at a high rate because men and women are too busy looking for love in all the wrong places. They are lowering their standards just to be in relationships nowadays. People are settling for less because they don't know any better. I have always heard the way you treat your mother is a representation of how you will treat your girl. Couldn't that also mean that the way you treat your father is an indicator of how you will treat your boy? By the way, I know most of you won't agree with me about this statement. You are under the impression that no one deserves as much respect as your father or your mother. To your credit, you are partially right. There are many people who don't deserve this respect at all, but I would like to think the love of your life at least deserves to be on the same level as your parents or guardian. The Bible tells us "a man leaves his father and mother and is united to his wife, and they become one flesh" (Genesis 2:24, NIV). The statement isn't referring to every man or woman who comes into your life. It is speaking to the love of your life. Our relationships are falling apart because men and women don't have their priorities straight.

I do believe we all can gauge our relationship potential by how an individual treats his or her father. I am not speaking of an earthly father. I am speaking of our heavenly Father who sits on high and looks down low. A lot of us don't realize our self-worth because we don't have relationships with God. The Bible, through the words of the apostle John, briefly explains the kind of relationship God wants to have with each and every one of us. The scripture reads:

> See what great love the Father has lavished on us, that we should be called children of God. And that is what we are. The reason the world does not know us is that it did not know him. (1 John 3:1, NIV)

I don't know about you, but these words comfort me. Ladies and gentlemen, we are all children of the King of Kings. This means we are royalty, and we shouldn't accept just any kind of treatment. We are better than that. I believe a lot of people settle because they don't realize they should expect the best because they were created by the best. Each of us deserves to be treated with the utmost respect at all times. God created us all in his image, and we should be treated as such. The bottom line is: enough is enough. Stop being someone's doormat.

The dating scene nowadays saddens me. I see so many individuals looking for love for all the wrong reasons. All of their issues stem from their self-centeredness. People are so afraid to be alone that they will just date someone due to convenience. They have a juvenile approach to relationships. Many people treat the idea of dating like a child treats a trip to the candy store. He or she picks his or her significant other based purely on impulse and cravings. There is nothing wrong with having a few Jelly Bellies, Haribo gummy bears, or my ex-girlfriend's favorite, Skittles. Having sweets in moderation isn't the problem. The problem is when you eat far too many.

As a youngster I had a very strong sweet tooth, and it landed me a date with the dreaded dentist. I can still smell the Boise-State-Broncos-blue dental dam that my dentist draped around my mouth with while she propped it open with a rubber stopper. I haven't forgotten about the ridiculously long needle, resembling a Michael Myers weapon, she used to numb my poor, unsuspecting gums. After this horrible ordeal, my mouth was numb, and I was unable to control the wretched saliva that poured from my lifeless lips. To make matters worse, I had to endure the dentist's drilling my sensitive teeth like they were a Chilean mine. The thought of the wretched sound of that high-pitched drill makes me tense up to this day.

Over the years I have noticed a change in my appetite, and that shouldn't come as a surprise to anyone. The apostle Paul wrote, "When I was a child I spoke as a child, I understood as a child, I thought as a child; but when I became a man I put away childish things" (1 Corinthians 13:11, NIV). After a few too many trips to the dentist, I learned to enjoy my fruits and vegetables, and I began believing the phrase "an apple a day keeps the dentist away." A diet based solely on sweets would have left my mouth and teeth in utter ruins and my body malnourished.

We can't walk around as if we are mere customers, picking lovers because they are sweet looking to our eyes. If this is the route we are going to continue to take, I believe we will continue to have Jay-Z's "On to the Next One" attitude. I am referring to the idea that you can get in and out of relationships for personal gain. Once you obtain what you want, you are free to go. Love is never meant to be a game of musical chairs.

I believe the reason our beautiful ribbons in the sky are starting to fade or have faded is related to the fact that men and women find love in all the wrong places. It took me a while to figure this out, but I found this answer in one of the most peculiar places: a 7-Eleven®, where I was forced to consume a minor dosage of country music. It was as if the sun, the moon, and the stars aligned as the sliding door opened, and I heard Johnny Lee singing his classic "Looking for Love." I fully understand if you are baffled by this answer, but I hope you also understand that at that moment, I was just as confused as you are now. The thing I learned is that love doesn't just happen. You can sit at home and pray about it day in and day out and never find even an ounce of it. You can sit and think about it all the time, and love will never find you. You can listen to the old wives' tale and do your best not to look for love and, well, it still won't find you.

Life is always about being in the right position to receive a breakthrough. Have you ever seen a guy with a woman and not know why he was with her or a woman with a man and you wonder, *How did she pull this guy?* Well, he or she happens to be with that person because he or she was in the right position to receive that person's love. That is why it is important not to sit at home feeling sorry for yourself, holding on to cassette tapes while others are listening to the likes of Pandora.com or XM radio.

As I noted earlier, the true reason why all hell is breaking loose in our relationships is we are finding love in all the wrong places. Yes, there are a number of ways we can demonstrate this. I believe that Johnny Lee's song touches on it so eloquently, and I want to show you what I mean. In the song the country singer states:

I was looking for love in all the wrong places
Looking for love in too many faces
Searching their eyes looking for traces
What I'm dreaming of
Hoping to find a friend and a lover
I'll bless the day I discover
Another heart looking for love
I was alone then no love in site
I did everything I could to get me through the night
I don't know where it started or where it might end
I'd turn to a stranger just like a friend

Now, doesn't this sum up your situation? There are so many of us who are still lugging around emotional baggage because we got overwhelmed by the love we found in the wrong place.

There are so many answers we can find in the words of Johnny Lee's song, and we are going to analyze the chorus a little bit more. In the very first line, he explains how he has been looking for love in all the wrong places.

For some of you, this subject doesn't register because you don't believe you were looking for love in the wrong places. You don't believe you found love in all the wrong places. Many of you are in disagreement with these words because you met your boyfriend, your girlfriend, or your spouse in the church or your place of worship. Maybe you found the one you love in the grocery store or a bookstore. Maybe you met him or her on eHarmony.com or another of the numerous online love sites. You could have even met him or her through a friend or at one of those speed dating events. The song does say "looking for love in all the wrong places," but don't let the emphasis on location cause you to miss your blessing. Looking for love in the wrong places can cover far more ground than longitude and latitude.

How are you looking for love in all the wrong places if you found him or her in the "right" place? For example, you may have met in your place of worship, but yet you ended up checking so and so out like you met at a gentleman's club or a male review. Come on, don't act like you don't know what I'm talking about. I guess I've got to spell it out for you. Don't act like you didn't find yourself tracing her silhouette with your eyes. Don't act like you didn't watch him walk outside and hop in that Aston Martin. Don't act like you didn't stare so hard at her chest, you could tell she was a C cup yet she had on a padded bra that gave the effect of a D cup. Don't act like you didn't marvel at his top-of-the-line suit, watch, or shoes. That's right, ladies and gentlemen, I caught you. You may have found this man or woman in the "right" place, but you were still looking in all the wrong places for love.

Many of us are guilty of this, and I am definitely included. Relationships are not turning out the way we want them to, and all hell is breaking out in them because we don't love someone for the right reason. We are looking for superficial things to love about him or her. I am not sure if this is ground-breaking news or not, but I still must fill you in. The size of a woman's brassiere might be quite enticing, and the size of her beautiful assets might grab your attention, but you will find yourself looking for new toys to marvel at

101

sooner or later. He might be able to buy you everything in the world, but in the end the one thing you need from him, he can't buy for you.

We all have to learn that love is not selfish, and love knows no status. All hell is breaking loose in your wonderful relationship because you don't understand that being in a loving relationship requires you to love someone unconditionally and wholeheartedly. Too many of us are hung up on storybook situations, and I must tell you to quit seeking a perfect union because there isn't one. You can't put two imperfect things together and expect perfection to come from them. That is not how it works. If you are looking for perfection, you are looking for love in the wrong place. You are looking for love in a dream world. I hate to break the news to you, but you need to wake up and smell the coffee beans. If you are looking for love to complete you as a person, you are looking for love in all the wrong places.

I know I have said a lot off of just the first line of the song's chorus, but we all must recognize why our relationships are falling apart and why we have to press the "reset" button ever so often. Unfortunately for you and me, our memories store everything whether we want them to or not. Sometimes we can't even tell that we possess these corrupted files in our mind. All we know is for some reason we can't get over the hump to love again. For some reason we find ourselves scared to death to love again. Once we check our bags in, we think all will be good, but we still keep finding the same brown grass. We are left looking for greener pastures, and every time we find them the grass seems to turn brown. What is the problem? It lies within each of us. Do we love someone because he or she loves us? Do we love someone to fill a void? Do we love someone because we truly love him or her?

A sad fact about love in the twenty-first century is that many of us love people for superficial reasons—for money, power, respect, looks, swagger, or what they can do for us—rather than because we want to love them. Remember, love is an action, not a state of mind. You could be in the state of loving someone, but you will never find a sign in your life saying "welcome to love." It would be great to meet the person who coined the term "I am in love." How can you be in an action? You can do an action, but how can you be in an action? No one says, "I am in thinking"; we say, "I am in thought." You can be so perturbed by someone that you hate him or her, but are you in hate? No. We must stop falling into the trap and selfishly looking for love because when you really love someone it is a selfless act.

Many of us have found ourselves believing in the notion of "the more the merrier." Don't sit there scratching your bum as if I am coming out of left field with this idea. Far too many of us do this, and yes, I am including myself. We are treating love like it is somehow the lottery, and we are all waiting to cash out. There are so many of us week in and week out making power plays. No, you are not the man or woman holding everyone up at the gas station, asking for two number twenty-twos, a thirty-six, a fourteen, and ten dollars on Powerball with the Power Play, but you are still playing the lottery. I know you have seen those people. Most of them are really not doing too well for themselves financially, and they are trying to invest in the wrong things. If you said, "Why don't you take that money and take it to Edward Jones or something?" they would be like, "Are you crazy?" These same people have the misconception that investing in the stock market is far riskier than trying to win the lottery. There is risk in investing in the stock market, and there an even larger risk in playing the Mega Millions, the Powerball, Pick Four, or any of the numerous lottery drawings. It is even hard to make a come up on those scratch offs. I do agree that in order to get high returns, you have to take big risks, but some risks we shouldn't take at all.

The same can be said for relationships. Many of us are out there talking to Darron, Michael, José, and what's his face or Keisha, Becky, Maria, and what's her face. In the process you find something good in all of them, and if you could just take this from Darron, this from Michael, this from José, and this from what's his face you would be happy. The same can be said for you men trying to take these qualities from Keisha, these qualities from Becky, these qualities from Maria, and these qualities from what's her face to have love by committee. This is not how love works. I agree it is a peculiar thing, and it is quite hard to be satisfied by one man or one woman, but it can be done once we quit trying to satisfy our hunger.

Just look at the United States. Our obesity numbers are staggering, and many people seem not to know why. Yet when you see what they put into their bodies, you know why. How are you going to go to McDonald's and order a supersized number three with a gigantic Coke, an extra order of fries, and two apples pies and not expect to feel or see the effects? Many people try to have their cake and eat it too, and that is where the problem lies. For the most part, you aren't being real with yourself or the people you love.

In the second line of the "Looking for Love" chorus, Johnny Lee expresses that the reason he hasn't found love yet is he was looking for love in too many faces and searching their eyes, looking for traces of what he was dreaming of. There are too many of us running around, looking for love, and I am here to tell you that love cannot be found. Love is not an inanimate object that is found under a rock, on a shelf, in a woman's blouse or skirt, in a man's wallet, or even in someone's eyes. I wish there was some indicator that love can be found, but there is none.

Many of us have all of these bags because we were looking for love in too many faces. Some of you are at the end of the road, some are in the middle of the road, and some are at the beginning of the road we call love. Some of you are neophytes, and you haven't learned that you can't find love. Love finds you. Just because you meet a good man or woman, it doesn't mean you all will fall in love. Just because your favorite color is red, it doesn't mean you will have a crimson and crème wedding. Just because both of you are the most beautiful things in the world, it doesn't mean you have any better chance at love than the rest of us. Just because you've got ten or eleven boyfriends or girlfriends, it doesn't mean your heart will fall in love with any of them or that any of them will fall in love with you.

All of you stuck in the middle are trying to decide whether you should turn around and go back to the beginning of the road or if you should keep on trucking. You know that being a player has not worked for you, but you don't like the fact that if you stop, you will have to come to terms with the thought of being alone. Those of you at the end of the road are either disgusted or have given up on love. Now you are a love hater.

Others of you have tried love; you love you some love, and you are very happy. You understand that love by committee leads to more drama than love. You know all too well that finding love in too many faces is the reason you couldn't find real love for so long.

Rather than looking for love, we should spend our time bettering ourselves and preparing ourselves for the future. If you want something from the store, you don't go and sit in the parking lot, expecting those items to just happen to end up in your vehicle. You have to take the time to get out of your car and walk through the sliding doors—which are great because they don't open until an object hits the sensor. Then they slide open. This means you must be in position for the sensor of love to go off, and at that time someone's heart will open. Your heart will open too when you and that person are in the right position.

It is hard to find love when you are searching for it. Honestly it is hard to find anything when you are looking for it. Most of us are quite impatient, and we can't find a thing when we are looking for it. I am the type of guy who loves listening to music on my iPhone, so I keep earbuds on me at all times. Just like all the people you know over fifty with those Bluetooths blinking in their ears all day and night, I have my earbuds in my ears. I can listen to music with them, and I can hold hands-free conversations with them on, so they are quite convenient.

Sometimes, when it grows close to the time for me to go to the gym and meet with my trainer or to one of the beautiful parks in Louisville, such as the great Cherokee Park in the Highlands area, I rush too quickly gather my shoes, clothes, and iPhone. I quickly put my earbuds in and put my phone in the pocket of my jogging pants or shorts. I pull the shirt I am wearing over the cords so they are not flopping everywhere. Then I run and grab my keys, and I am ready to go burn some calories.

One day I found myself unable to find my earbuds and I knew my workout was going to suck. The music keeps my mind off the pain of an eight-mile run or the many things my trainer takes me through at the gym. On this day, for whatever reason, I couldn't find them, and I was about to lose my mind. Then, as luck would have it, I walked in front of my mirror, and in my ears were my earbuds. I laughed to myself, got out of the house, and got my workout in.

That is what is wrong with so many of us. We are out there rushing, looking for love. Oftentimes, when we go for long stints without being in relationships, we become concerned that something may be wrong with us. I hate to admit it, but in my life I have friends and family who love to remind me that I am not getting any younger, and I should be married with children as we speak. Am I the only one who has friends who invite them out to the movies, dinner, and various locations with their significant others? Who wants to be the third wheel? Come to think of it, maybe my friends do this to try to motivate me to go out and find a nice young lady with whom to settle down.

Have you ever been so busy looking for something that you ended up over-looking the very thing you were looking for? Sounds like my earbuds example, doesn't it? Sadly many of you, like me, have found yourselves doing the same thing in your love lives. You have searched high and low, yet you have not found him or her. That's not how love works, though. If you are not careful, you may find yourself alone because you don't look in the direction of someone who doesn't fit a particular tax bracket, doesn't have the phy-sique you are looking for, or doesn't fit profile of the man or woman of your dreams. That is why I suggest that someone who is looking for love should focus on getting himself or herself ready for love. Then, when it is all said and done, you will be ready for him or her when he or she comes into your life. He or she won't be Mr. or Mrs. Perfect, but with just the right amount of work he or she can become Mr. or Mrs. Just Right for You.

The reason your attempts at love have been failures is you have been looking for love in all the wrong places, and it is quite all right. Maybe you didn't know you were looking in all the wrong places because music, media, movies, and magazines taught you that you should selfishly seek what you want to get out of a relationship. There isn't a foolproof solution to finding love, but there is a way not to be a fool while seeking love. I believe the biggest question we must answer will cover why we keep looking in the wrong locations.

I hear you whispering to yourself, and I promise that you won't have to ask this question anymore. The answer to why we keep looking for love in the wrong places is we don't possess the maturity to know any different. Understand when I say *maturity*, that doesn't mean I am counting how many candles you have on your birthday cake; some people can have a mere sixteen candles and are fully aware of what love is, not to mention what it is all about. Then there are others who could put so many candles on their cake, it would be easier to go out and buy number-shaped candles instead. Or is that just me? The saddest fact about love is that people are childishly making decisions of the heart.

Indeed relationships are failing because of people looking for love in all the wrong places. They are also falling apart because people lack the maturity they need to succeed in matters of the heart. Another byproduct of this immaturity is that men and women are going into relationships for selfish reasons rather than being selfless. An old man once told me that in order for me to be truly happy in a relationship, I should forget myself and do my absolute damndest to please my woman. If I don't do so, I may find myself in hell on Earth because hell knows no fury like a woman scorned.

In R. Kelly's smash hit "When a Woman's Fed Up," he explains, "There ain't nothing you can do about it," and this line is so true. As a young guy, I laughed at the man, but now, looking back, I must agree with him whole-heartedly. While in college I unfortunately got to take a few trips to hell's kitchen, and I am thankful to say I lived to fight another day. Unfortunately, though, I found myself needing some sound rehab.

All women are beautiful, but there is nothing more beautiful than a happy woman. Happy women are more willing to go the extra mile than unhappy ones. The same can be said for men. If a woman goes out of her way to en-sure a man is happy, he is more apt to make sure his queen is experiencing the utmost happiness and respect. If he doesn't there needs to be a serious discussion. I am not saying do things for your special someone so he or she does them for you. I am saying do special things for your special someone so he or she feels special because you love him or her. If this is reciprocated, there will be a healthy bond and years upon years of happiness. There will be issues from time to time, but that's part of it. With a lot of love, little prob-lems shouldn't affect the greater good or your lifelong union.

Throughout this chapter we have discussed why our relationships are not working out the way we want them to. We have discovered in this discussion that men and women are looking for love in all the wrong places. Also we discussed why many of you keep finding yourselves seeking love in some-one's wallet, in someone's eyes, in someone's physique, status, etc. This list goes on and on. Many of us have found ourselves trespassing in the wrong places, looking for love because we lacked maturity.

Surely you didn't fall into the same trap the forty-year-old crazy, sexy, cool singer Chilli of TLC fell into. Did I forget to mention she's a radiantly beautiful songstress? On her reality show, *What Chilli Wants*, she told the world what she looks for in a man. Chilli explained, "I was built to be someone's wife." However, in order to find this man, he must measure up to her standards. She doesn't want him to drink, smoke, eat pork, or have more than two baby mamas. He must be fine to the eyes, with at least a four-pack. Last but definitely not least, the man of her dreams must possess a really massive personality in his boxer briefs.

I admit some of her list makes perfect sense because if you are not a drinker or a smoker, why would you want to be involved with someone who does either of those things? If you don't eat pork, I guess it would be much easier not to date or marry someone who does. We aren't even going to bother to discuss the baby mamma/baby daddy drama that is consuming the dating scene. My problem is the fact that she believes she deserves a man who is fine as all get out and has a really massive personality in his jeans. I believe physical attraction is important, but looks aren't everything. Sooner or later those looks fade away.

When I held this discussion with a number of friends on Facebook, a couple of them brought up a subject that is near and dear to my heart. It is, in my opinion, one of the main if not the main reason why our relationships don't seem to work. Many of us continue to search in the wrong places and find it hard to mature from childish things because we are not putting faith into our relationships. Many of your relationships are falling by the wayside because maybe you have someone who on paper would seem to be a seasoned, mature individual, but he or she isn't acting his or her age. Maybe it's not him or her, and sadly it is you. Mother has already clapped her hands, stating, "My baby is all grown up." You have a great career and at least one degree, and you have a real mature, grown-up look about you, but you are still stuck in the candy store. You understand that when you were a child, you spoke as a child, you understood as a child, and you thought as a child, and now you are all grown up, and you know you are a man or a woman. Maybe you even think like a man or a woman but for some reason, when it comes to issues of the heart, you can't seem to get past looking for a woman far more beautiful than Kim Kardashian or a man with an account larger than Donald Trump's. This is indeed a sign of immaturity, and I know that faith will help you and your significant other see past these things.

I hope you understand I am not suggesting you seek someone you can't find attractive. The Lord said he wants us to multiply, and frankly I can't multiply with a woman I can't stand to look at. I am not saying drive out to your nearest homeless guy or gal on the highway and see if you have that romantic spark. All I want you to do is understand why these two qualities are important to you. One day in the not so far future, Kim Kardashian's beauty will pass, and another man will come along with a sexier financial résumé than Bill Gates'. Love is something that endures all if you work at it. It won't be perfect, but it will be worth the effort.

Many of our relationships have fallen off the tracks because we listened to the ill-conceived notion that opposites attract. I admit I wanted to believe this fact, but it was yet another attempt at trying to link science up with mankind. When discussing magnetism, opposites do indeed attract one another. If you were to take two magnets and put them together, you would learn rather quickly that the north poles of each magnet will push each other away. When you put the north and south poles together, they will pull one another closer until they are bound together. Now, if we were to take this matter to nature, we would find another story. Many of our relationships do not work because we don't belong together. Maybe on paper he or she looked like a prime candidate, but as time went by you noticed he or she was not a good fit.

The book of Deuteronomy tells us, "Do not plow with an ox and donkey yoked together" (Deuteronomy 22:10, NIV). The problem nowadays is that men and women have lists of qualities, but most of them aren't important in the whole scheme of things. You have found yourself like the beautiful singer of TLC, with a long rap sheet of nothing. Every time you come across someone, this is what you do: You found a man or woman who goes to church. Check. You found a man or woman who has a neat appearance: Check. You found a man or woman you can talk to. Check. Shockingly you found a man or woman who doesn't have any baby mammas or baby daddies. Check. He or she doesn't drink or smoke. Check. This man or woman is beautiful, and you can take him or her home to Daddy or Momma. Check. This person has an awesome physique. Check. This beautiful person has a bank account of which Oprah Winfrey and Christy Walton could only dream. This handsome man has a bank account that Carlos Helú and Bill Gates could only imagine. Check. Now you think, *This wonderful individual is all that, a bag of chips, and some extra dip*, right?

Through conversation this lovely person lets you know he or she doesn't believe in God, and you do. Rather than letting him or her go, you decide to start a relationship. You do this even though you are a believer, and you are the first person in the sanctuary and the last one to leave. All is good in your mind because you don't have faith anywhere on your list. In the end your relationship goes up in smoke, or you raise children who don't know which way to turn. On one side you believe they will be baptized in the eternal fire because your children and your significant other do not believe in the god you believe is the savior of mankind. On the other side, your children go to worship with you, and your significant other is viewed as an outsider who will perish because of his or her beliefs. That will not be a good look whatso-ever. The worst thing that could happen is your relationship may influence you to no longer be a strong believer.

Understand that the ox and the yoke represent two individuals in a relation-ship. Since I was a young man, my mother always told me to make sure my love interests and I were equally yoked, and this scripture tells us why. The problem is this scripture was not based on twenty-first-century ideals, so many of you are left asking what in the world an ox and a donkey have to do with you. Well, ladies and gentlemen, an ox is a very obedient animal, and a donkey is a very stubborn one. When a farmer is trying to plow his field in a straight line, he needs an animal that is obedient. If you were to mix an ox and a donkey, there would be a major problem. Two oxen would continue to walk till told otherwise. When they were told to stop, they would stop. If they were directed to go left or right, they would go in that direction because they are obedient. and if one ox stopped, the other ox would stop because that is their nature.

For a donkey the game is different. Donkeys do what they want to do. They work well together because they will be stubborn together, but if you put one with an obedient ox, sooner or later the ox will follow the donkey. Now the farmer wants the donkey to go right, but the donkey is going left, so the farmer will go in the wrong direction.

The same can be said for our relationships. We start off being like the obedient ox, who just so happens to find a donkey who matches our list. While we are going one way, our chosen partner is going the other. As a result we end up going left when the Father is trying to get us to go right. Now we miss our blessings because we are stuck with this donkey. I am fully aware that society has made faith and religion a point of argument, and for the past couple of decades there has been an attack on the power of being a believer. Understand I am not trying to speak to you as a perfect individual because I have my faults. I could probably write another book called *If I had only not…* or *I Shoulda, Coulda, Woulda but Didn't*. You would be amazed by how many times I've fallen short of the glory of God, yet I am still here, alive and well, to tell my story to each of you.

I hope this conversation helped you as much as it helped me. I have been guilty of looking for love in all the wrong places. I remember when I was younger, people told me not to look for women in the club, at fraternity parties, or on the stage of a gentlemen's club. They told me if I wanted to find a good woman, I should look in places like church, the grocery store, a bookstore, or a coffee shop. While this might sound like good advice, it is not always true. You can find a person in the right place and still be looking for love in the wrong places.

True love cannot be defined by her Coke-bottle frame, his abs, her monthly income, his job title, her beauty, or his handsomeness. How can you say "I do till death comes" if you are making lifelong decisions based on temporary situations? Sooner or later that Coke bottle will look more like a Pepsi can, and his washboard abs will look more like a keg. Your love will not pass the litmus test of endurance if for some reason one or both of you is still steering through life and taking childish exits. As children we all did childish things, but a relationship requires a grown man and woman to work out. Your relationship should not resemble one from *Degrassi High*. In the end you need to do your best to keep the faith and steer clear of donkeys. Be obedient on your path, and learn to love life. It's not always perfect, but it is always a blessing to have another day to live and love.

Like · Comment · Share

PART II
Every Little Step We Take

⚜

6

Is Love as Easy as One, Two, Three?

Richard Rowland Jr.

Do you want to know why our relationships, marriages, and friendships keep dying? I believe it's because we keep ignoring the warning signs. Why do you think we miss the warning signs or ignore them?

Like · Comment · Share

Comments

Kamesha I think our relationships in the United States are in trouble because people don't respect boundaries anymore.

Carl Richard, I could probably go on and on about this topic. Number one—there are very few examples of positive relationships: People actually believe they are supposed to raise kids by themselves. I am not saying it cannot be done, but a little boy becomes a man by being exposed to men, not random boyfriends or uncles. There needs to be a man in the house. A woman can raise a boy, but she can't teach him to be a man.

Number two—temporary friends: Most people are put in your life for a season. Some seasons are longer than others, but most people are temporary. A lot of folks are so concerned with keeping it real that they hang on to friends who are no longer beneficial. I still keep in touch with a lot of folks from Murray State, but even some of my closest college buds are no longer my friends because we grew apart. They aren't pedophiles or cannibals, but we have different interests now.

Number three—marriage is viewed as an accessory: The importance or the seriousness of marriage has been diminished. People treat their marriage like a jacket that has gone out of style. Sooner or later it is time to toss it and get another. I wish people had to apply for marriage like they do gun permits because everybody should not qualify.

Number four—last but certainly not least, Christian morals and values have been tossed aside. Keep God first.

Let me add that I'm not trying to single out guys. The same rules can be applied to raising girls (women have to be the example there), but I think the breakdown of society is directly related to the breakdown of family, which is directly related to most males' inability to lead. This is directly related to boys who have no idea how to lead because they never learned from quality male role models in the first place.

Rikki Marriage and relationships aren't supposed to resemble the relationships we had in middle school or high school. As adults we are supposed to become one with the people we love. Two people can't do that if they don't know themselves. Having someone in your life because of what he or she can do for you or just to say you're not alone leads to having to accept things you shouldn't have to. When you find someone who is on the same page as you about God, family, finances, lifestyle, and the future then you have the chance of a lifetime. No one can agree with you on those issues if you're not honest with him or her about who you are and what you want. More so, you can't be honest with someone if you don't know yourself. Nowadays communication is broke down completely. Turn off the television, phone, and computer and talk only to your mate, and ask yourself if you have enough conversation to last an hour or a lifetime.

Treone First, I have to agree with some things that both Carl and Rikki said. On the flip side, I honestly believe one can take the initiative of learning from the mistakes of others so they know what to do in the future. My example of that: A lot of us (including me) grew up in single-parent homes and may not have always seen healthy, thriving relationships. Couldn't we learn what to do or not to do by watching what was going on around us? With the "temporary friends" thing, I know that problems can arise when we put permanent expectations on seasonal people or relationships. (I first heard that in one of the Madea plays.)

Naomi Some warning signs are more serious than others. The reality is people can get blinded by emotions to such a degree that major problems are minimized only to become big time issues down the line. I knew a guy who lied about smoking for months. I asked why he smelled like smoke, and he said it was because he took his break with people who smoked. Sadly I was so in love, I didn't think anything of it. But when he finally spoke the truth about his smoking, I remembered he would rinse his mouth with Listerine when he came in from work, and at his best friend's place he would have to say no when they offered him cigarettes. Hindsight is definitely twenty/twenty. He was a nice guy, but I didn't feel I could trust him anymore. If he would lie about something as small as this, what else was he lying about? What else would he lie to me about?

January I think sometimes we are blinded and sometimes in denial. We see what we want to see and believe what we want to believe. Say your boyfriend or girlfriend is cheating. You know in your head that he or she is, and the signs are right in front of your face. Yet you choose to ignore it because you're so blinded by love, and you keep telling yourself excuses like "I'd rather be with somebody than be single," "I can't be-lieve what other people tell me," or "We've been together so long, and I know he or she loves me." These are just some of the many excuses people will tell themselves because they're in denial and choose not to see the warnings signs.

Marissa I think we look past the warning signs we do see. In other cases we underestimate them, and we don't see the future implications these warning signs are preparing us for. Some people want to come off so high and mighty that they remain proud and ignore the warning signs on purpose because they don't want to fail. All of us have to get past this, though. If we are having issues in our relationships, I believe it is important to try counseling. By the way, I think counseling should be proactive rather than in reaction to something. I believe this will build the communication skills needed to help the couple grow closer to-gether. In essence, that tighter bond could have a profound effect on the relationship. This will make working through problems possible rather than being clueless.

Treone My initial answer would be to look at the foundation of the re-lationship. What is it based on, and how much work and effort were put into making sure it was solid? I've noticed that relationships based merely on emotions, passions, or impulses aren't really successful in the long run. Relationships in which the people didn't take the time to grow as friends first before becoming more have a hard time too. You don't really know the person or what you're getting yourself into. People are so caught up in the right now that down the line isn't even considered.

I would also say that the motives for being in a relationship are impor-tant. Why are you with ____? Why should you be with__? What about your friendship makes you believe that you two could possibly be more? My personal understanding of relationships—i.e., dating—is that you're looking to see if this is someone you could potentially marry and spend the rest of your life with. Others don't see it that way, which is why they get with someone they'll be with only while it's summer or until their money runs out. Even during the "just friends" phase, you do have to pay attention to the red flags. I think (some) people who say, "I didn't know they were like that or had that in them" are lying. They saw it before but chose or choose to overlook it. (I'm aware that some people aren't good liars though.) It's amazing what people will endure just to say they are with someone.

Like · Comment · Share

Richard Rowland Jr.

Have you ever found yourself in a relationship where you knew you didn't receive the love or support you deserved? This problem can arise as a result of three separate reasons. For starters, many of us are guilty of holding on to relationships beyond their season. Second, we have issues in relationships because we find ourselves on different levels of under-standing, which creates a rift. Last but not least, our relationships fail because as couples we don't fully understand the fundamentals that make love work.

As a child my mother and father taught me that the hardest part about growing up was letting go of what I had become accustomed to in order to move on to something I hadn't yet experienced. Even though as a young man I didn't fully understand what they were hinting to me about, I have carried it with me to this day. Now, looking back on it, I am fully aware of what my parents meant. In all of our lives, we have things we never want to let go of and people we never want to leave behind. Jeffrey A.Wands, author of *Another Door Opens*, stated "that too often we let relationships drag on because they've become familiar and we seem to have invested a lot of time and energy into them even though they may be difficult or detrimental to our emotional well-being."

121

Alexander Graham Bell, the man who invented one of our most coveted methods of communication, said years ago: "When one door closes another door opens, but we so often look long and so regretfully upon the closed door that we do not see the ones which open for us." This is a bad habit that many of us carry on. Admit it: it is easy to get overwhelmingly comfortable with the familiar. An online contributor to the Cool Blues consortium of articles included an article that reads:

> Once a king had a problem, he became very happy on any happy event and became extremely sad on sad events. It felt as if he could not control his emotions rather his emotions appeared to control him. Being quite disturbed by his extreme behavior, he asked his officials to do something about it. One of his officials was very wise, he wrote a sentence on the ring of the king "This time shall pass too" and he asked the king to read it whenever he became too happy or too sad. Now whenever the king was overjoyed, he would read this line and he felt that this happy time would be over soon. When he became sad, the king would read this line and realize that the sadness would not last forever and he remained in control of his emotions. (Haq, *Small Talk: This Time Shall Pass Too*)

My friends, we all must understand that whatever state we are in shall pass. We cannot lose sight of this valuable point. There will be times when we are inspired to laugh and other times in this life when we are compelled to cry. Neale Donald Walsch explains, "Your life is going to change…with you or without you. Life is very impartial. It doesn't care whether you were part of creating change, or just an uninvolved bystander" (2).

Since life is going to happen, I would rather be a participant than a bystander who watches it pass me by. Sadly many of you don't realize you are uninvolved bystanders in your lives. Your problem is that you are still regretfully looking upon the door that has been closed for quite some time, causing you to miss new doors that have been opened for you. It is human nature to grow accustomed to things and to be apprehensive of things you haven't yet experienced. That is why men and women have a hard time letting go of old friends who don't have places in their lives. That is why we all sometimes struggle to get over our exes. Many of you would rather deal with the mess he or she brought into your life than gamble with someone new. Why? The reason is simple: people are more content with being comfortable than with experiencing something fresh. The problem that arises is that over time, the thing you have grown accustomed to is changing.

Dr. Muhammad Wasif Haq further argued, "Reality is, nothing last forever, nothing is permanent." Everything in our life has a season whether we want to accept this fact or not. This next statement should come as no surprise, but sometimes relationships are up, and sometimes they are down. It takes maturity to realize there is a time for everything in a relationship. The Bible says:

> There is a time for everything, and a season for everything under the heavens:
> A time to be born and a time to die
> A time to plant and a time to uproot
> A time to kill and a time to heal
> A time to tear down and a time to build
> A time to weep and a time to laugh
> A time to mourn and a time to dance
> A time to scatter stones and a time to gather them,
> A time to embrace and a time to refrain from embracing
> A time to search and a time to give up
> A time to keep and a time to throw away
> A time to tear and a time to mend, a time to be silent and a time to speak
> A time to love and a time to hate
> A time for war and a time for peace
> (Ecclesiastes 3:1–8, NIV).

Ladies, stop holding on to relationships that don't prosper you, and take back your power. Fellas, stop holding on to relationships because you don't want to be labeled a quitter. Something each and every one of us must realize is if we have done all we can in a relationship, and we discover that someone is still not good for us, we must let him or her go. We have got to love ourselves enough to let him or her go. This takes great courage. Once we understand this, you will make the best decision of your life. Stop thinking you can change him or her because you can't change anyone. The best thing we can do for our health and sanity is know when to walk away. The mistake many of us make is we hold on to things of which we should be letting go.

Sadly men and women stay in unhealthy relationships because they fear being alone or starting over. Maybe you stay because you believe he or she will change. I hate to be the bearer of bad news, but most people don't change, and others won't change. You will likely find out this point the hard way if you stay long enough. Maybe he was a man who couldn't be trusted, or maybe she is a woman who no longer is in love with you. Yet and still, you find a way to stay. Admit it: you are paralyzed by fear of the unknown. Now you are stuck asking yourself, "Do I stay or do I leave?" The fact of the matter is you just need to let go and walk away. Dr. Maya Angelou said it best: "When someone shows you who they are, believe them." It would behoove you to understand that "holding on to a bad relationship is like holding on to the bumper of a car while it drags you along, all you have to do is let go, and alleviate the pain" (Margo Hudson).

Have you ever been in a relationship that has gone through periods of up and down, sweet and sour, and high and low? Something you can expect to encounter in any relationship is growing pains. It is just part of the loving process. There will be times when you feel completely satisfied and others when you feel you aren't getting the love you deserve. Problems like these stem from couples not being on the same level of understanding. How can you and your significant other ever expect to reach a level of understanding without having meaningful conversations? How is any of this possible unless both of you are patient with one another?

Rev. Darrin Moore, pastor of the historic Greater Centennial A. M. E. Zion Church in Mount Vernon, New York, gave a sermon that explained this situation to a tee. He utilized an experience he had in his own life to paint this illustration. Pastor Moore spoke of one occasion when one of his friends, a fellow minister, went to upstate New York to visit him. This was the first time his friend had been to Mount Vernon, so Rev. Moore wanted to pull out all the stops. He planned on having the man meet him at 6:00 p.m. at a beautiful hotel downtown, which happened to have a great restaurant on the forty-second floor. To ensure that the other minister reached the hotel with no problem, Mr. Moore gave what he thought were accurate directions. Notice I said, "what he *thought* were accurate directions."

On the day that Pastor Darrin and his friend were supposed to have dinner at the hotel, the time for dinner came and passed as Darrin patiently waited. At 6:10 p.m., he received a text from his friend explaining that he was having a difficult time finding the restaurant. Darrin then sent a text with the same directions he had given the other pastor previously. The visiting minister sent back a text explaining that the directions to the restaurant were great, but for whatever reason the elevator he was on wouldn't take him up to the forty-second floor. Every time he attempted to get there, the elevator would stop on the eighteenth floor.

After hearing the visiting pastor's problem, Pastor Moore realized the issue. The problem wasn't the directions, because his friend was downstairs in the hotel. The dilemma wasn't the elevator because it was working just fine. The pastor could not get up to the forty-second floor because he was taking the wrong elevator. All the visiting minister had to do was walk across the hotel lobby to catch the appropriate elevator, which would take him to the forty-second floor, where he could enjoy dinner with his friend. After Pastor Moore's friend had established where he was and the problem he was experiencing, Pastor Moore was able to lead him up.

Why are our relationships failing? They are falling apart because we all lack patience; we are deeply frustrated, and we have grown sick and tired of being alone. Admit it: a lot of you would have lost your minds if you were in the same situation. This same thing happens in a lot of our relationships. When we meet someone, we are excited, and we invite him or her into our life. Usually when people meet, they are not on the same level. Some of us are already waiting on the forty-second floor while others are trying to find their way there. Many of us miss out on great relationships because we aren't patient enough to give someone the time needed to reach the right floor. Not to mention we have to be prepared to communicate with each other. Many of us make the same mistake Pastor Moore made—he gave his friend great directions to the hotel but neglected to tell him how to get up to the forty-second floor. I am quite sure that there were signs in the lobby that directed him to the appropriate elevator, but we can't expect everyone to notice signs. Everyone gets bogged down with life from time to time, and we sometimes look right past the obvious. More than likely the elevator the visiting pastor was on had buttons that went up only to the eighteenth floor, but he didn't recognize the situation because he was busy trying to make it up to the forty-second floor.

Sure, Pastor Moore could have gone down to help his friend, but he recognized the easiest way to get his friend up to his level was to lead him. In a relationship it is never a good idea to stoop down to your partner's level. If you have to do so to make the relationship work, there will be a problem. Just mark my words. There is a reason why you are on the level you are on.

Relationships are completely about balance. That is why communication and patience are important to a couple. The minister and Pastor Moore wouldn't have enjoyed a beautiful meal, looking over the beautiful city, if either of them didn't communicate or didn't remain patient. Many of you right now are suffering from rifts in your relationships because you both don't have the same level of understanding. The easiest way to come to a level of understanding is to communicate.

What would happen if we didn't communicate? Not communicating with our significant others is the equivalent of getting on an elevator and not hitting one of the buttons designated for the various floors. How can you ever expect to reach your destination if you don't hit the button? How can you expect to reach a level of understanding if you and your significant other don't communicate? A lot of times, our relationships don't reach their full potential because we neglect to hit the button.

The important thing we all must understand is that perception is reality. We have to hit the button to reach the forty-second level because our perception is everything. There are things that people on the forty-second floor can see that people in the lobby can't see. What people perceive is usually what they believe, and it is based on what they see, hear, and think. That is why we have to hit the button. If he or she is on the forty-second floor, don't wait another minute. Hit the button. If you don't hit the button, you could miss out on the love of your life.

Due to perception, Dom Cobb, played by Leonardo DiCaprio in the movie *Inception*, lost the love of his life. In the film Cobb is a thief who is skilled in the art of extracting valuable information. He has the ability to perform illegal corporate espionage by entering the subconscious minds of his targets using dreams. Cobb's wife, Mal, played by Marion Cotillard, also possessed the same skill and she assisted her husband on quite a few information heists. Unfortunately Mal got caught up in the fantasy world and couldn't decipher fantasy from reality. Mrs. Cobb committed suicide accidentally because she believed the world she was in was the dream world she and her husband had created. She leaped to her demise because she thought she was in their "inception."

A lot us have done this as well. We have created dream versions of our relationships, and we believe they have reached the forty-second floor, but they have not. Or we believe that we're both our in the lobby, and we are actually forty-two floors apart. Not to mention we think we are at a level of understanding. Sadly we have had relationships end, and we have been forced to wake up from our dream worlds. Many of you have been trapped in this inception you have created and now can't decipher what is real and what is fantasy. It is important to understand that our perception is our reality.

Also don't get distracted by all of the other buttons. They represent the various options and opportunities that come our way. We have to make sure we have our priorities straight. If he or she is on the forty-second floor, we have to hit the button marked with the number forty-two. Being in the same building isn't enough. How are you going to enjoy what the forty-second floor has to offer if you don't hit the button? Remember, what we perceive is what we usually believe, and that is all relative to what level of understanding we are on.

The one thing we can learn from Pastor Moore's story is that hitting the button isn't enough. His friend hit the button, yet he didn't end up on the forty-second floor. Relationships are failing each and every day even though the couples are communicating. What seems to be the problem? Ladies and gentlemen, we can talk twenty-four hours a day, and this doesn't mean we will reach a level of understanding. Darrin Moore's friend was on an elevator, and he hit a button, but there was a problem: he wasn't on the correct elevator. A lot of our relationships fail because we are too busy to pay attention to the little details. This brother walked right past the concierge, the map of the lobby layout, and the various signs that would show him how to get up to the restaurant. Doesn't that sound familiar? How can we ever expect to reach a level of understanding with our significant others if we can't find the right way up?

We will never reach the forty-second floor if our significant others aren't patiently communicating with us on how to reach the special elevator on the other side of the lobby. Perception is our reality, and sometimes I can't see the things you see. We make the mistake of thinking he or she will see it.

Pastor Moore gave his friend great directions to the restaurant but didn't include directions to the elevator that would take him to the restaurant. He assumed his friend would make his way up to his level just fine without his help. We can't assume he or she is going to reach our level of understanding if we don't tell him or her how to get there. We are all built and wired differently. It is not fair to anyone to think he or she should know XYZ. Instead of being disappointed that he or she got lost on the wrong elevator, do him or her and you a favor. Give him or her the directions to your heart, and don't skim over any details. If Pastor Moore had given his friend good directions to both the hotel and the restaurant inside, his friend probably would have made it upstairs for dinner at six o'clock. There is a possibility that he would have gotten lost, but the probability is much smaller.

Look back on your relationships for a moment. Did you ever wonder why your significant other wasn't meeting your needs? Did you ever ask yourself why you weren't meeting his or her needs? The problem is he or she has ended up on the wrong elevator, and you need to tell him or her how to get to your special elevator. He or she needs to lead you to his or her special elevator. Sometimes in our relationships, we can be so close yet so far away. The reason is we all have to learn how to love one another. Far too many times, we all make the mistake of trying to do it our way, and that's all it is to it. A relationship is not about us doing it our own special way, and it is not about our mate doing it his or her own special way. We all have to learn how to express our love to our significant others the way they like to receive it. If you want your partner to be more affectionate, guess what? You have to let him or her know you want more affection. If you enjoy words of affirmation, you have to communicate that fact. Just because you like receiving gifts, it doesn't mean he or she enjoys it as well.

We all have our own ways of giving and receiving love. That doesn't mean we shouldn't be in relationship with certain individuals. That just means we have to be patient and communicate how we like our needs met so we can come to a level of understanding. Most if not all of us won't end up in relationships with mind readers, so talk about what you like and dislike. Learn about what he or she loves and doesn't love. It will help out a lot in the long run. There is no need for either of you to end up on the wrong elevator. Mature couples understand this fact, and that is why they have worked as long as they have. They understand that communication is one of the important parts of a relationship.

Many couples make the mistake of not communicating in the beginning. The earlier you and your significant other communicate, the sooner you can be on your way to reaching a level of understanding. If Pastor Moore's friend had communicated that he was having a problem getting to the forty-second floor before 6:10 p.m., Pastor Moore could have led him to the elevator earlier. Rather than speaking up later, please bank on speaking up sooner. Relationships are about balance, and that means we must lay strong foundations. This is not an option. And we can't expect to build strong foundations if we aren't on the same level. Why not? Because you can't even begin to build a strong foundation if the ground you are building on isn't level.

Before you build anything, you need to choose a lot. You can't select the bedroom suite, drapes, or appliances until you investigate the soil conditions. If we try to build a foundation on the wrong surface, the implications could be disastrous. In the book of Matthew, Jesus taught a parable about a foolish builder, which reads:

> Therefore everyone who hears these words of mine and puts them to practice is like a wise man who built his house on rock. The rain came down, the streams rose, and the winds blew and beat against the house; yet it did not fall, because it had its foundation on rock. But everyone who hears these words of mine and does not put them into practice is like a foolish man who built his house on sand. The rain came down, the streams rose, and the winds blew against that house, and it fell with a great crash. (Matthew 7:24–27, NIV)

Relationships are falling and have fallen because many of our couples have been like the fool. We have built our relationship on sand. Trials and tribulations came, and the relationships fell with great crashes. If a relationship is meant to last, it has to be built on the solid rock. A relationship has to be built on faith.

Not only do we have to turn our focus to the building blocks of the relationship; we must also dispel the myth that monogamy is a thing of the past. It is my fear that healthy, strong, loving relationships will soon be on the endangered species list. Or worse, this kind of relationship will become extinct altogether. In my opinion there is an attack on monogamous relationships. There are quite a few people willing to contend that human beings were never meant to be in monogamous relationships. There are others who are willing to argue that a truly fulfilling, monogamous relationship between a man and a woman is impossible because we are too different.

Wouldn't it be a shame if the only place you and I could see a truly loving, monogamous relationship was in a Smithsonian exhibit? Fear not, ladies and gentlemen. All hope is not lost. There is great potential for beautiful, loving relationships even though the odds seem impossible. Love is a deep well with an endless amount of water, and we can continue to fill our buckets till we have had enough. Just realize that the well is our faith, the crank is our communication, the rope is our patience, and the bucket is our heart.

How do we shore up our foundations to ensure our relationships will grow? In order to make sure that a foundation is strong, we have to build it up block by block on a level, solid surface. The first block we must lay in the northeast corner represents our understanding of who we are and what we desire out of this life. The second blocks we must lay are two of the most important blocks in the foundation. They force us to question our needs, our expectations, and what we want out of life. If at this point any of you is left scratching your head, I suggest you rethink your current situation. I am not asking you to throw in the towel, but I do feel you and your significant other must start anew to make it work. It is not fair to you or your significant other if you are unable to figure out what you want out of life. If you can't decipher how you complement one another then you are back to square one, or in this case you are back to block one of the foundation. For all of you who have established in your minds what you want out of life, and you realize how your significant other complements your life, you can now move on to the final set of blocks. These final building blocks of the foundation represent having a level of understanding with our mates.

I realize making a relationship work could come down to a matter of understanding the fundamentals. The problem is men and women get bogged down in looking for the big things in life and don't appreciate the small things. Lawrence D. Bell said, "Show me a man who cannot bother to do the little things and I'll show you a man who cannot be trusted to do the big things." Those "little things" I have simply called the fundamentals are the ABCs and one, two, threes of the relationship.

My mother and father raised me to the sounds of the musical classics. My mother did not allow me to watch BET or MTV. She believed that music videos had negative and risqué messages. I can remember the first time she pulled out one of the Jackson 5's LPs and placed it on the player. At the young age of four, she gave me the opportunity to hear a song that became one of the most cherished songs of my childhood. There was something about Michael Jackson and his four talented brothers. What is the song I speak of? It is none other than the 1970 smash hit *ABC*. It helped me gain an understanding of what makes up the basic elements of love.

What about this song taught me about the small things of love? For starters, it taught me that communication gives all of us the ability to close the gaps between us. Most relationships start out the same exact way. In the beginning we all find ourselves worlds apart from our mates, but through unleashing the power of communication we can begin to get on a level of understanding.

At this moment some of you might be finding yourselves saying, "I hear what you are saying, but how do the words from the song *ABC* teach me about communication? How can I apply them to my relationship?" The chorus of the song reminds the love of the singer's life of the basics of spelling and arithmetic. That is something we all must keep in mind when we are dealing with love in our own lives. How are we ever going to learn to love one another if we don't know how to fulfill the most basic needs of our partners? Love is a very peculiar matter, but we shouldn't make such a big fuss of it that we can't reap the benefits. Too many of us believe love is quite an impossible entity, yet these five young men from Gary, Indiana, professed that love is as easy as counting up to the number three.

Do you remember way back when you first started learning about what love was? This was the time you experienced your first taste of rejection. It also could have been the time when you first experienced a victory in the wild world of dating. Ladies and gentlemen, we are all products of our environments and our pasts. We can't control where we came from, and we can't control what has already been done. The only thing we have control of is our attitude. It is important for us to take time to reflect on where we learned our positive and negative views on love. Many times this is the place where we began hoarding the emotional baggage we carry around to this day. Keeping a positive attitude and learning from our past situations can help us in our future endeavors.

There comes a time in all of our lives when we have been guilty of trying to love someone without knowing the basics. This is not an embarrassing matter. It is a fact of life. Moments like these are how we learn. As children we learned how to walk first by crawling, then by falling all over the place until one day we were able to stand alone and take our own steps. Through those times we learned how to balance ourselves and how to use our legs to carry ourselves across any surface. As children we couldn't speak in words, so we learned to cry. Over time we began trying to say words, and it all came out like gibberish, but through time and effort we learned how to hold conversations.

The same thing can be said about love. We started out by learning that we love our parents and then we made friends with anybody and everybody. Over time we learned everyone wasn't our friend and that the opposite sex isn't quite as yucky as we'd thought—that they are actually a very beautiful creation. After learning this incredible tidbit of information, we began wanting their attention. And over time we learned what it means to love someone as opposed to liking him or her.

The last five lines of the song *ABC* give a broader scope on love. How? First and foremost we all must conjure up some confidence. We can't go into love not being confident about ourselves or our relationships. That is why at the end of the song, these young men confidently sing, "Love is as easy as counting up to three." Treat love like the Internet.

All we have to do is insert a name and click "L" "O" "V" "E." I agree if you are thinking this is rather simplified. Understand if you love someone all you really have to do is make the decision to love him or her every day. Love is a choice. Stop missing out on love because you took the fun out of it. It is definitely a serious matter that shouldn't be taken lightly, but that doesn't mean we have to be on a level-ten alert at all times. Love can be very fulfilling and very fun. I admit finding Mr. or Mrs. Right can be quite difficult, and I want you to know if you continue searching for him or her you will be wasting your time. There is no such man or woman. What it all boils down to is we must understand what the basics are. Once we understand that, we have to realize that we can do nothing without understanding two very important keys to any relationship. Those are communication and patience.

Next the Jackson 5 explained that love is as easy as singing do, re, mi, which are some of the first notes any singer learns. Don't let the unfamiliar cloud your thought process because if you haven't noticed by now, I am going to do my best to teach you a little something something along the way. These three words—do, re, mi—in music are very important for remembering the tones and positions of notes. How can we ever find harmony in our relationships if for some reason our attitudes are out of pitch? I hope no one is scratching his or her head, but I am going to explain this more in detail. Have you and your significant other ever been frustrated by one another not because of what one of you said but because of how you said it? Let that marinate overnight. Pop that puppy in the oven for four hours and then cut and serve.

Imagine you and your significant other are having a conversation when all of a sudden, you ask him or her in a sweet tone to do you a favor. On the other hand, he or she answers in angst while giving you the stank eye. You get all bent out of shape and you find yourself getting an attitude at him or her. That is why it is very important for all of us to communicate with one another about what works for us and what doesn't. This will allow us and our significant others to have long-term harmony.

There will be times when problems arise. These will be far and in between if we are on the same level in the same building. Again, love is impossible to have more abundantly if we find ourselves on the wrong elevator that won't help us reach the forty-second floor. Beethoven couldn't have created notable works of musical art had he not had a basic understanding of do, re, mi. We cannot expect to enjoy a harmonious relationship unless both of us are playing at the right pitch, at the correct tone, in the exact position. In the end your knowledge of this will allow your relationship to be a simple melody that seems so easy to everyone else. No matter how you want to cut it, love requires hard work. But last time I checked, anything that is your passion is not actually work. It is an enjoyable experience through the rough times and the great times.

I believe that a number of us are guilty of overlooking one of the most important elements of a relationship, and this is the reason we can't begin to take off. This element is the key to our having the ability to reach that ribbon in the sky that Stevie Wonder sang about so long ago. It is all fine and dandy when you and your partner have the golden rule down pat, or you all understand that in order to be happy you must first make your significant other happy. Those are two very valuable points that will allow you two to have the potential for a healthy, long-lasting, and loving union. However, if these two items are standing alone, you will end up with your relationship in shambles and your heart broken once again.

What is this element of which I speak? What is the most fundamental element? Some of you will applaud me for making this point, and others will be shocked when I say this. The most important element is your personal view of yourself. I hope this doesn't come as a complete shock. That's right, ladies and gentlemen, I am giving you the right to look out for the man or woman who is in the mirror. We all have the right to look out for number one. If number one isn't happy in a relationship, number one needs to talk to number two about the problems.

Why is your personal view of yourself the most important element? Because it will affect who you allow into your life. Your view of yourself will affect how you let someone else treat you and how you treat him or her. If you don't believe in yourself, how are you ever going to believe in someone else? If you don't love yourself, how are you truly going to love someone else unconditionally? Just take a moment and let those questions percolate.

A lot of you had a hard time getting advice from someone who knew what they were talking about because you couldn't get past your own insecurities. You were in a horrible relationship, but you stayed in it far after the love was dead and gone because you didn't think you could do any better. Now you have closets full of emotional baggage, and you don't know what to do with all of the pent-up frustration and anxiety. Many of you are still hurting because you chose Mr. or Mrs. Right Now because you didn't think you were good enough for your Mr. or Mrs. Right. Your self-image was so low that you didn't think he or she would give you the time of day, so you went out and dated someone you had no business getting with. You saw the dangers of this relationship a mile away, but you thought this was your only chance at real love.

It is quite impossible for any of us to find a happy relationship if we aren't first in tune with what Katt Williams refers to as our "star player." The concept of being in tune with your star player basically means an individual must truly love himself or herself for each and every strength as well as for every flaw. Every individual's responsibility is to know his or her boundaries. It is very critical to be in tune with your star player.

There is no doubt in my mind that all of you have heard the phrase "you are only as strong as the weakest link." Just imagine that your relationship is represented by a chain. One end of the chain represents you, and the other end represents your better half. Both ends are pulled apart, and it takes an extremely strong tug to break the links in the chain, so it serves as a strong example of your union. This means that both ends of the chain or both individuals in the relationship are in tune with their star player.

Now look at the example one more time. The two ends of the chain are pulled, but this time one of the links breaks with a very weak pull, though the rest of the chain remains strong. What good does that do us? It doesn't do us any good at all because as we already said, a chain is only as strong as its weakest link.

A relationship is only as strong as its weakest link as well. Each person in the relationship must hold up his or her weight, to ensure there is a strong potential for growth. Everyone has to be in tune with his or her star player and must know his or her role. There is a reason why he or she wants to be with you, so bring your best foot forward. There is no need to miss out on love because you are so busy trying to get over something that happened years ago. We shouldn't miss out on love because we don't value our own self-worth. Before you bring someone into your life, I suggest you work issues like that out so you can step forward anew.

Surely no one reading this book right now would ever think of hopping into and out of relationships because they can't stand the idea of being alone. I know that all of you are better than that, right? Actually I am fully aware that a number of you reading these words just endured breakups, and you have already found someone new. I am not saying that is bad, but the heart does need a little time to heal. Did you hop into it because you knew there was a possibility for a healthy, loving relationship, or did you hop into it to fill a void? If it's the latter, you are just one of the many men and women who have left others with emotional baggage. You don't have a problem with understanding that you are one of the fundamental elements of the relationship; your problem is that you believe the relationship is about you.

It is quite apparent that the dating pool is saturated with individuals who are quite self-centered, and due to this a rift has formed between an individual's view on fantasy and his or her view on reality. Let that percolate for a little bit. We all have been witnesses to plenty of examples of men and women who have found them selves walking on cloud nine, with their heads among the clouds. Or worse, they have had their heads stuck deep in the sand, like ostriches. There is nothing wrong with enjoying your temporary high from your romantically induced euphoria. Most if not all relationships begin with some kind of romance or fantasy stage. Many of us are oblivious to any of the flaws our significant others display until the love serum or the honeymoon period wears off. And then the chinks in the armor are in full display.

As people grow more comfortable in their relationships, they seem to develop a bit of peripheral blindness as well as a touch of amnesia. In these instances many people seem to mimic the mythical story of a scared ostrich that put its head in the proverbial sand, as written by Pliny the Elder. People tend to put their heads in the sand because they don't want to allow themselves to see the wrongs of their significant others. This defense mechanism leaves them vulnerable to heartache and pain.

I fully understand that finding someone to love is hard, but keeping the one you love is an even harder task. And the hardest task of all is making sure you didn't just settle. All I ask is that you keep your eyes focused on the signs and set on the prize. I am sure at this very moment a number of you are staring at this page blankly, asking yourself over and over again what the prize is. If you must ask, I guess it is only right for me to answer. And the prize is you. We are each a prized gift for that special someone we have in our life till the alarm clock wakes us no more.

In the end loving someone is as easy as knowing our ABCS or our one, two, threes. Healthy, loving relationships don't have to be a thing of the past, but we all have a responsibility to ensure they don't become extinct. We must have good self-images and truly love ourselves before we can ever love someone else.

Love does not hinge on the big things, but it does hinge on the little things. Please make sure you and yours go back to the basics, when love was fun and sweet. Reminisce on those times all the time, and remind yourself that love is a choice you must make every single day. You literally must ask yourself, "Is this relationship worth fighting for or not?" The moment you decide it is not worth fighting for is the very moment your links in the chain break. You stop holding up your weight, and the stress and strain the world puts on couples will buckle you down, and problems will soon follow. There is no need to run for the hills or hide amongst the crowd. There are a multitude of reasons relationships fail, and it is up to us to understand this fact before involving ourselves with someone else.

The more basics you cover in the beginning, the stronger your foundation will be. And having a strong foundation means your relationship will have somewhere to find strong footing. Every day will not be sunshine, and at the same time every day will not be heartache and pain. We just have to reminisce about the building blocks of our relationships. When we combine all of these basic elements, we can forge strong bonds.

Like · Comment · Share

7

What's Love Got to Do with It?

Richard Rowland Jr.

I've been asked what the fundamental issue of relationships is. The fundamental issue is that we are missing rungs on our ladders to matrimony. People, if we skip steps in the process of love, like skipping rungs on a ladder, we will have a great fall sooner or later. If we build strong foundations and take calculated steps, we will have healthy relationships.

Comments

Nia There are certain steps you just don't leave out or skip when you want to experience a deeper love in your relationship. This deeper feeling of love will be impossible to achieve if certain steps are not taken.

Cowann True words, but some folks are operating with stepladders— going through the motions, rushing things, and realizing when they're on the top, they still aren't at the right level to reach their happiness.

Michael Love and commitment are two very important rungs on the ladder to real love. Men and women must realize we need not only a commitment to the relationship but commitment to working things out. We truly have to love one another to be patient enough to talk things through and listen to what is said.

Yolanda Zig Ziglar said, "Court your wife till you are called home and your personal and work life will be balanced till you reach heaven."

What do we do nowadays in our relationships? We stop courting or dating one another. We stop working on our relationships. We even quit making our significant others feel as loved as when we first uttered those three words: "I love you." We must work daily to let the ones we love know they are loved, appreciated, needed, and essential to our success in this life. If we keep God first, he will provide the person he has in store for us. One rule of thumb we all must live by is we must stop looking to fulfill our needs in relationships. We will never be satisfied if we do so. We will continue to fail at finding our mates with a mentality like that. Love God, and keep him first, and everything you desire will be given to you by the one who knows you best: God.

Stephanie Yolanda, girl, I couldn't have said it any better. I agree with you. Those words of wisdom you have given are very beneficial to all of our relationships. It almost seems that after we say "I love u," we seem too complacent in our relationships. The appreciation of that partner starts to dwindle. Sadly the communication even takes a swift turn to the left. I believe men are supposed to be the utmost gentlemen, and women should be ladies. It's all in our actions. Court each other. I love that so much. That's something my father would always remind me as a young girl. He always said, "Honey, let a guy court you."

Like · Comment · Share

Richard Rowland Jr.

What does love have to do with it? It has everything to do with it. Love is a decision that requires patience to make it work. We have to spend time on the things we value. If we spend no time on our relationships, how can we expect them to grow?

There are no shortcuts to real love. We must be willing to commit ourselves to the slow, painstaking work of loving each other day by day and year by year. Mark Zuckerberg said, "There are no shortcuts to success. A lot of building a company or a product like Facebook is just about determination and believing that you can." The same can be said about building a strong relationship based on true love, which is just about our wills and our faith that we can stick it out through thick and thin.

Building a long-lasting relationship is a very hard test and an enormous responsibility. In chapter six we learned that in order for us to build a strong foundation, we must build it up block by block. As a matter of fact, we have to construct our love meticulously in order to dwell in it for the rest of our lives. Anyone who wants to experience a successful relationship must understand that love is a process. Every little step we take with our significant other is important. We can't expect our love to withstand all of the hellish storms that come our way if we don't concentrate on every single step we take.

Love is a home, a refuge against the storm. And like any house, it requires a strong, lasting foundation. To build one every couple needs to take certain steps. In fact there are eight steps involved in building a house that lasts. All of us should be aware of the first step of any relationship: communication. In the last chapter we discussed its importance. In order to build a home, you have to talk to a bank or mortgage company to make sure you are able to get money to complete the house. In the same fashion, before we start building our love, we must have an internal conversation. We have to figure out whether we have the maturity needed for a successful and long-lasting relationship or not. Strong relationships require large amounts of maturity. Without it we will not erect a love that lasts.

Once we have reached a certain level of maturity, we should be able to find a suitable building lot. Remember, strong relationships are built on faith. The Bible tells us, "If you have doubts about whether or not you should eat something, you are sinning if you go ahead and do it. For you are not following your convictions. If you do anything you believe is not right, you are sinning" (Romans 14:3, NIV). That is why we must plan to suit the lot rather than get our plans and then look for a lot to suit them. Each of us has our heart set on a specific plan. But will it be built on the solid rock or sand? If we base our love on material things and our significant other's physical attributes, there will be a problem. Sooner rather than later, our relationship will wash away because it was built on sand. A relationship based on the love of our Lord and Savior is meant to last. "Delight yourself in the Lord, and He will give you the desires of your heart" (Psalm 37:4, NIV)

Don't be afraid to dream. Just because our love is based on the Father, it doesn't mean we can't have fun with it. It doesn't mean He won't bless us with the woman or man of our wildest dreams. We each have the right to imagine who our significant other will be. Realize we each have our own individual expectations for our significant other. I don't know about you, but I want a woman who fits me. If our dream mate is made to fit the building lot we spoke of earlier, I don't see there being a problem. The only way we can figure out if our design is correct is to test it. During the building process, potential homeowners have the ability to test their ideas on 3-D software. This helps them put their ideas into perspective and gives them an opportunity to try out different concepts, layouts, and designs without running into a large bill. After they have created their desired home, they must take the design to the architect.

A lot of us have large emotional bills. I understand why. We live in a society where people say, "By dating around, you learn what you want in a marriage partner" (Ludy, 84). If you would take a moment and be honest, you would agree that dating around didn't prepare you for holy matrimony. In fact this practice has set you up for divorce (Ludy, 84). A considerable amount of us suffer from emotional debt, and we are unable to afford our dream love. God never intended for our hearts to be toyed with. He doesn't want his sons and daughters to waste their time with multiple short-lived relationships. That is why we can take our love interests to God, and he will put them into perspective for us without our accumulating emotional baggage.

Once the architect has created the official plans, it is time to deliver them to the developer, who controls many aspects of how a home is built in a subdivision. Most subdivisions have particular building schemes. Some have restrictions on how homes can be built in them. In our lives God is not only the grand architect but our developer. In his word he has given us the restrictions about love that we must follow in order for it to be worthy enough to be in his kingdom.

What restrictions? Let's take a look at a few familiar passages. In the words of our creator, we all must "submit to one another" (Ephesians 5:21, NIV). Not only that but "wives, submit yourselves to your own husbands as you do the Lord" (Ephesians 5:22, NIV). "Husbands, love your wives, just as Christ loved the church and gave himself up for her" (Ephesians 5:25, NIV).

Notice God's first restriction was that we submit to one another. First and foremost, this word of submission doesn't have anything to do with leadership. God is asking us to recognize one another as equals. To take this a bit further, verse twenty-two asks women to submit to their husbands as they do to the Lord. Again, this doesn't mean a man has full control of his wife. This submission is actually a request for reverence. A woman must respect her husband at all times. And last but not least, men are asked to love their wives as Christ loved the church. Realize that in the word, God never intended for man to lead his woman; he wanted him to love his woman as Christ loved the church. That means when a man sets his heart on a woman he desires, he is willing to set her apart from all the other women. He seeks companionship with only her, with the goal of holy matrimony. She is not just a fling. He loves her with a purpose.

When the developer accepts the architect's plans, it is time to make an offer on a lot. Every time you put an offer on the table, it is subject to financing.

WHAT'S LOVE GOT TO DO WITH IT?

This is the time when you put your money where your mouth is, and at this juncture of the process talk is cheap. If you are unable to receive the financing needed to be approved for a lot, you will have to try again next time.

Remember what we said earlier in this discussion: we have already selected a suitable lot. We are going to build our home on the solid rock. Whenever you are building for a particular subdivision, the architect takes into account its various restrictions. Our grand architect works in the same way. During this part of the process, we are just preparing ourselves for whomever our significant other will be. Whenever you see the beautiful lot you want in the subdivision, you make an offer because you see where you want to live. The same can be said for when you see him or her. When this individual comes into your life, you must be ready to make an offer. When you make the affirmation that you want to start getting to know this individual, you make an offer to the developer. At this point in time, you should focus on building a friendship so you can get to know him or her.

During the building process, it is imperative that all the various companies and entities give you cost estimates on how much their services will be throughout the project. That way at the end of the project, there shouldn't be any surprises. In our relationships we too must receive some estimates, which we refer to as goals. We must have tactful communication with our significant others. We need to know their short-term and long-term goals. In order to prepare for our futures, we must know what their views are on relationships. Last but not least, we have to know how these men or women feel about us. No offense to Steve Harvey or his book, *Act Like a Lady, Think like a Man,* but men and women alike need to ask these questions, not just women.

After we have received the cost estimates, it is time to arrange for suitable financing. More than likely the mortgage provider will require we have appropriate insurance when construction begins. It is important to make sure your home is protected in case of fire, theft, and anything else that can affect its

145

value. Similarly we must be prepared to take our relationships to the next level. There will come a time when we need to commit to each other. We have learned about the other person's goals, and now we should know if we really want to accept his or her bid. If this man or woman is someone you can see yourself building a deeper love with, then go ahead and start the construction process. It is not time to hop the broom, but it is time to arrange for construction to begin. Understand that many of us make the mistake of thinking about marriage far too late in the relationship phase. When we meet someone we are romantically interested in, we should already start a design in our mind. Remember, we build our love to the lot, not the lot to the individual. If we are patient, the developer will make sure that we build accordingly.

There comes a point in the eight steps when it is time to build. Before we can start the construction, we must get a building permit from city hall. Understand we don't get the permit until after both the developer of the subdivision and the architect have approved the plans. The developer gives you a plot plan to go along with the building plan. A plot plan explains to city hall where your house will be in the subdivision.

Now comes the time in your relationship when you take it to the deepest level it can go. The grand architect has designed the plan, and the developer has approved the design for construction. It is up to each of us to take the next step. Before this process can continue, we must get a marriage license. In the process of building a home, there must be a building permit before you are allowed to begin construction in a subdivision; in the same way we need to get marriage licenses before we begin construction on our families. I realize that in this day and time, some of us have made mistakes along the way and have missed a few steps. Ladies and gentlemen, we can't skip steps. When we skip steps, we impede the process and receive unneeded stress. How many of you have headaches because of some of the choices you have made? Lord knows I need an Excedrin thinking about all the mess I have put myself through, trying to skip steps to find someone to love me.

When you finally receive the building permit, you will also receive a list of conditions that must be met. In the case of the house, some beams may need to be engineered or the soil may need to be tested. In our love lives, we are given lists of conditions as well. Receiving the marriage license is just part of the story. On our wedding days, we will receive traditional sets of conditions that must be met unless we decide to write our own. What are the conditions that must be met? They are known as the wedding vows. In the process each man and woman agrees to take his or her significant other as his or her wedded wife or husband. The agreement is made to have this individual in his or her life from that day forward, for better, for worse, for richer, for poorer, and the list goes on and on till the candidates for marriage proclaim they will cherish this love till death do they part. We must meet these conditions to make sure we all strive to live happily ever after. The beams must be engineered to ensure the house is ready for living. The soil must be checked to see if the lot is ready for building. When we profess our vows to our lifemate, we are finishing the final test of our love.

Step eight of this great process has to happen throughout the building process. Waiting for the permit allows time for you to get organized. It gives you the opportunity to start arranging for the contractors, surveyors, framing crew, and excavators to come in. That way each of them has a timeline, and you have one as well. These individuals are very important parts of the construction scheme. Everyone must be on the same page to ensure that the building is erected appropriately.

Back in chapter one, we discussed the importance of building a team. Knowing who we run to in stormy times is very key to our success. When the house is being erected, it is important to contact the electric company from time to time, to arrange for the usage of temporary power. Sometimes this process can be time consuming, and you could ask a friendly neighbor to lend you his or her power for a small fee. In our lives we too must contact the electric company to receive our power. Our Lord and Savior, the creator of electricity, is the only source we need to tap in to. He holds all power in his hands, so why wouldn't we want to tap in to that? He is that friendly neighbor next door, willing to offer you all the power you need to finish the project.

Several times people have asked me, "Richard, how will I know when a relationship is from God?"

Eric and Leslie Ludy explain, "We need to develop a team. Our team should be made up of godly people who can keep us accountable to our commitments, pray with us, and provide a refreshing outside perspective on the ups and downs of our journey through life" (Ludy, 187). With a good team there isn't a need to "figure things out on our own" (Ludy, 87). We don't have to figure things out on our own because we will have a support system that wants what is best for us. Leslie Ludy explains, "one of the beautiful things about having teammates is that they provide an outside perspective on a friendship or a relationship. They can see the things that we are sometimes blinded to" (Ludy, 191). That is why having the appropriate men and women to run to is so critical to building a love that lasts.

Does it make a difference? What if I don't follow these steps? Are these questions you asked as you read the eight steps above? The answer is" it's up to you. I can't speak for you, but I have learned in my life that not following the steps has caused me a considerable amount of heartache and pain. All of my life, I have searched for real love in my way, but I haven't found it yet. There is a possibility that I have been in the presence of true love, but the fact of the matter is I honestly don't know what I am looking for. French author François de La Rochefoucauld said, "True love is like a ghost; everyone talks of it, but few have met it face to face."

The idea of love reminds me of an online article I read called "Following Instructions." In the article John G. Nichols speaks of an occasion when his wife pulled out an old Rubik's Cube that had been boxed up for quite some time. Have you ever fiddled with a Rubik's Cube? This is a very difficult toy to get a grasp of, but once you have the pattern, it is simple. The Rubik's Cube can become so cumbersome that it forces whoever is playing to pull out the directions. Clearly, ladies and gentlemen, if you can't get the Rubik's Cube to match up for you, follow the instructions.

Admit it: for many of you, love is just like this Rubik's Cube. The peculiar nature of love is awkward. You have taken several cracks at it, but you haven't broken through yet. So what have you done? You've followed the same plan as John Nichols, and you've dug out the instructions to prepare for one more chance.

The directions explain that "the Rubik's Cube is solved one layer at a time" (Nichols). Isn't that how love is? In order to build a love that lasts, we must first construct a strong foundation. Many relationships fall apart because people ignore this step. People forget the fact that the root word in *boyfriend* or *girlfriend* is *friend*. Friendships are normally not developed overnight. Building a strong relationship with your potential significant other will shore up a strong foundation. People who are friends generally have things in common that bring them together. How do they find out about these similarities? Well, simply put, they talk about them. If you and this individual are unable to build a friendship, there is a problem. Like the Rubik's Cube, real love is created one step at a time, and we can't rush it.

That is a problem for many of us. We realize it is very important to build a friendship first, but we want to expedite the process. We have followed the steps thus far, and we have created a great friendship with a man or woman. Now we believe we are ready to take our friendship to the next level. To our dismay our relationships have failed over and over again, and we don't know why. We assume something is wrong with him or her. Right? John G. Nichols had the same problem when he was trying to match the squares of his Rubik's Cube. He followed the instructions and diagrams showing how to move the cubes in the middle layer. He would almost have it correct when the colors would get messed up. He figured the instructions must have been wrong, for he followed them very closely.

British reformer Thomas Hughes stated, "Blessed are they who have the gift of making friends, for it is one of God's best gifts. It involves many things, but above all, the power of going out of one's self and appreciating whatever is noble and loving in another." Building a strong love that lasts requires that we learn how to go the extra mile for our significant other. Love is full of compromises and sacrifices. Men and women have this fact all wrong. We spend our lives seeking our Mr. or Mrs. Right, and sadly we don't find him or her. Every relationship will have its ups and downs. That is why it is essential to have a strong friendship. There is a saying I learned when I was younger: a true friend is someone who knows the song of your soul and sings it back to you when you have forgotten the words. Don't our significant others need to know the songs of our souls? Don't we need to know the songs of their souls?

Not only do our significant others know our songs, but so do the men and women we run to. At least they are supposed to. What good is it to run to someone who doesn't know your song? Having people who know you for who you are will serve you well. Building a love that lasts is quite a huge undertaking. Step eight in the construction process is essential. Those people who know our songs main roles are to keep us in check, to ensure we experience love that lasts. In many cases this man, woman, or group of people recognizes issues before the relationship even begins. They may very well notice that our potential significant other is a great fit for us before even we realize it.

Trying to find a love that lasts can be a very frustrating time in your life. I have heard on several occasions that love don't cost a thing, but after dealing with a failed relationship I feel so spent. Don't you? When you truly care about someone, you do your best to make him or her feel loved. If you really love someone, you are willing to put a lot of time into it. Wouldn't that mean love costs something? Yes, it does. Sadly time is something you can't get back.

On many occasions people find themselves in relationships with people they can see themselves with for the rest of their lives. I have been down this oh, so familiar road a couple times in my life. I followed the steps I laid out to the tee. At least I thought I did. In each case the woman and I had an incredible friendship, and we could talk about everything. We loved spending hours upon hours together. We both knew each other's song, and we knew it well. We could even finish each other's lines before the other had a chance. She was the yin to my yang, and I was the hot to her cold. Then life happened. Doesn't that sound familiar?

In John's example about following the Rubik's Cube instructions, he explained that the one thing he learned was he "could not follow the instructions while carrying on a conversation. He had to concentrate to prevent mistakes." The main thing he learned from this was that he had to follow instructions "with understanding." Isn't that what we need to do? We need to learn how to love our significant others with understanding. We have got to learn how to love them in a special way. El DeBarge used to sing a song called "Love me in a Special Way." In it he sang: "Love me now/'cause I'm special/not the average kind/who'd accept any line/that sounds good."

I realize that from time to time, life can become quite cumbersome, but we can't lose sight of the prize. We cannot just give the men or women in our lives some average kind of love because they are special. Building a love that lasts isn't an easy task, and it requires us to focus. We have to make sure we don't take our significant others for granted. Aldous Huxley argued, "Most human beings have an almost infinite capacity for taking things for granted." So what does that mean? That means we have to work hard to make sure we don't underappreciate the loves of our lives.

In the case of the Rubik's Cube, I would be willing to agree with John and say "it is a complicated toy and the instructions are complicated as well." After he understood the instructions, he was able to "place all the cubes in their right places" (Nichols). I don't know about you, but I want to make sure my love is in order. I want everything to be in its right place. When a Rubik's Cube is complete, each layer matches the other. The same thing can be said for a love that was built to last. In order for your love to work, you and your significant other have to match. That is why it is so important for us to be equally yoked.

Please don't be afraid to dream. The grand architect wants to design the love of our dreams for us. We just have to be prepared to follow the steps it takes to ensure that it lasts. Skipping steps can be very detrimental to the building process. I realize that being patient is the furthest thing from our minds since we live in a fast-paced world. If we expect love to be our refuge from the storm, we have to be prepared to wait for it to be built properly. What does love have to do with it? The way you and your significant other prepare your love has everything to do with it.

Like · Comment · Share

8

Why Can't We All Just Get Along?

Richard Rowland Jr.

It is said that men and women are of the same species, yet when they communicate they seem like different species. What are we to do if we are unable to communicate with each other? How do we bypass this issue?

Like · Comment · Share

Comments

Treone I believe we have to use the tactic of trial and error. When something doesn't quite work, try something else and see what happens. If this doesn't work out, hone your inner little engine that could. Remember: "I think I can, I think I can, I think I can" until you make it happen. Don't be afraid to continue trying new things until you find something that works out.

Richard Rowland Jr.

What do you do if you never hit the mark, Treone? I believe in trial and error as much as the next man, but that could take forever. What do we do when someone loses patience?

Treone Richard, *never* is a strong word to use because in theory it denotes that you have exhausted every possible option (someone's in grad school, lol). Patience is the key because we won't always hit the mark. That's where understanding and consideration from the other person will also play pivotal parts if they see that you are putting forth a genuine effort.

Greg The only ways to bypass these problems of communication are time and patience. We need time to get to know that person, and we need time to learn their quirks and nuances. Everyone must understand that communication is a key component to any relationship. Love should be the number one thing. Notice I said it "should be." If we truly love our mate, love is very important. When you really care about someone, you are willing to do anything to make the relationship work.

Like · Comment · Share

Richard Rowland Jr.

How can we expect to build a strong bond without communication?

Greg Honestly, Richard, that is a great question. I can't imagine that a strong bond would come without it. Without it, that means the foundation won't be laid correctly. If this happens then there will be a problem. In times like these, miscommunication occurs. There is an incident or a situation that adds to the breakdown of communication. If the relationship starts wrong then the bond will be unable to become established.

Shenika The key to communication is studying and learning about your significant other. It should definitely go both ways. Taking the time to study and learn your mate should give everyone a better understanding. Furthermore it should better prepare you for him or her and vice or versa. The ability to learn your mate, boss, or even friend is very important. We have to learn what our mates need. Do they need soft hugs, or do they need some kinky loving? It is our responsibility to do the math. If he or she starts an argument for attention, what are you going to do about it? It is up to both the man and the woman to learn their relationship inside and out.

Chandra Girl, I hear you, Shenika. You are so right in so many ways. Any man who wants to get in my life will not only have to talk with me but he is going to have to learn my body language because I am a quiet person. As a woman I owe my man the same respect. We all should know or make honest efforts to find out what makes them tick, what touches makes their toes curl, and last but not least if they crave attention. Do they need to be in the limelight? This learning process is lifelong. We should continue to learn about our mates as long as our lives have breath. With that in mind, understand that communication is a continuous cycle. The question becomes "are you in it to win it, or was it just a waste of time from jump?"

Amanda Since miscommunication and misunderstandings will happen, I believe everyone must be mature in the situation. I believe there are lessons to be learned from problems in a relationship. None of us is perfect, and we never will be. That is why we study our partners more during a storm to get to know them even better. We will never reach perfection, but we can sure try to get a step closer. Each and every one of us will miss a hint or not notice our significant other's body language sometime, and there will be a subtle sign that will be ignored. Even though these times are frustrating, these are the times when we can learn about each other.

Johnnie The way we bypass this issue is by paying close attention to our significant other's strengths and weaknesses. It is vital to learn how to communicate with one another. Gaining that understanding is of the utmost importance. If two people in a relationship don't learn to communicate, that brings up three scenarios. 1) The individuals in question will get used to one another and learn how to master the art of mind reading, making the relationship work. By the way this is highly unlikely. 2) The disagreements in the relationship continue, and the couple gets majorly stressed out. 3) Last but not least, this is the scenario I see happening more than the other two. The relationship ends, and both people end up looking for replacements.

Like · Comment · Share

Richard Rowland Jr.

"With our divorce rate hovering somewhere between 50% and 60%, is it not reasonable to ask if men and women really can get along" (Rudov, *Can Men and Women Really Get Along?*) Not to mention "thirty percent of Americans have never been married. This is the largest percentage in the past 60 years," says the US Census. To make matters worse, Kreider and Ellis, renowned Census researchers, explain in chilling detail that "profiling the marital experience of the population as of 2009 shows that first marriages which ended in divorce lasted a median of eight years for men and women overall. The median time from marriage to separation was shorter—about seven years" (Kreider and Ellis, 85). These numbers point out that men and women can't get along, right? You know what they say: the numbers don't lie. These numbers are rather stifling, but we cannot bank on them, ladies and gentlemen. I have nothing against the researchers or their findings. The problem is these statistics do not give enough details for us to infer adequately that this is an indication that men and women can't get along. This brings us full circle and back to the initial question. Why can't we all just get along?

Before we can even begin to take a stab at why we can't, we must understand if we can. This disturbing question was posed two decades ago by

Rodney King, who is best known for his involvement in a police brutality case with the Los Angeles Police Department on March 3, 1991. Mr. King uttered these very words in an interview in response to the Los Angeles riots, which were sparked by the acquittals of four LAPD officers who were videotaped beating him.

A number of you may have chuckled when you saw the name of the chapter because you remember the likes of Martin Lawrence, who made this a catchphrase on his show. Every time he posed this question, it was humorous, but please don't let the humor cause you to miss the seriousness of this question. We indeed have a problem, and Houston can't do anything about it. We all need to figure out if we can get along. In the conclusion of his interview, Rodney King stated confidently, "We all can get along. I mean, we're all stuck here for a while. Let's try to work it out. Let's try to beat it."

That is something we need to do. We need to try to work it out, and we need to try to beat it. Why can't we get along? I believe men and women can't get along because we believe it should be easy to work as a team. People point out the Census bureau's numbers and act as if the dynamic of a relationship has changed. Rochel Holzkenner, the writer of the online article "Why Can't We Get Along: Understanding the Male/Female Dynamic," contends that "making marriage work has never been easy. Marriage is not for the feeble and weak-kneed. It takes a lot of focus and resolution to get along." Not only are marriages not for the feeble; neither are relationships. We have to come to grips with this idea. Just because two people are in love with each other, or just because they care about each other, it doesn't mean it's going to be easy.

While reading Rochel's article on the male-female dynamic, I was introduced to "a Talmudic scholar and Jewish mystic" who addressed this very question. The funny thing is this man lived five hundred years ago. Like many of you, I questioned "what a sixteenth-century rabbi would understand about a modern relationship, one based upon equality and individualism?"

Rochel explained that this Jewish scholar knew "more than we'd think." The Maharal, which is how he is referred to, examined a scripture from the book of Genesis. And It reads: "it is not good that man is alone; I shall make him a helpmate opposite him" (Genesis 2:18).

Holzkenner states, "After creating man, God decides that it's time to create a woman, and before doing so he expresses the dynamic of their relationship: 'a helpmate opposite him.' This description is a classic oxymoron; a 'helpmate' implies assistance, while 'opposite him' implies resistance." The Maharal believes that these words explain God's intent with marriage. He wrote, "A person can be a helpmate to his parents, for example, but shouldn't ever stand to oppose them. But a woman, who is of equal value and importance to a man, will help him and oppose him." Now, let these thoughts marinate for a moment.

What in fact was the sixteenth-century rabbi explaining? Let's analyze the words from Genesis 2:18 once more. "It is not good that a man is alone; I shall make him a helpmate opposite him." Why was it "not good that man be alone"? Why is it not good for man or woman to be alone today? Each and every one of us enjoys our moments of solitude, but I have yet to meet an individual who truly wants complete seclusion. That is not the way men or women are wired. A common vice among men and women is that we will settle for something to rid us of the feeling of loneliness. That is why some people hit the bottle or the pipe and even hold on to relationships of which they should let go. In some cases, such as my own, people can go for large amounts of time without having interactions with the opposite sex. That all changes when we hang out with a friend who is married, we go to a dinner party, or we go out to a lounge and see couples interacting with each other. That is when we notice how alone we are. In this instant loneliness consumes us. Does that happen to you?

I imagine this is the same thing that happened to Adam. He was fine living alone. God had blessed him to live in paradise. He had anything and everything he needed, or so he thought. Then God gave Adam the responsibility of naming all of the animals, and this was the instant when Adam realized he was alone. The lions came in male and female; the doves came in male and female; and every other animal came in male and female. Could you imagine being this man? He was given the great task of naming every animal, and in the process he realized he was alone. While being responsible, he felt incomplete even though God had made him whole. He never made a fuss, though. He didn't get disgruntled and quit doing his work. He kept being obedient to the creator.

Does that not sound familiar? Many of you are in the same place as Adam. You have been obedient. You aren't grumbling, but deep down inside you feel alone and incomplete. Every which way you turn, you see families or couples expressing love to each other, and you want that. I'm willing to argue that you need that. That is one of the greatest gifts the creator gave us.

In the scripture it never says that Adam asked God for someone. It says God said, "It is not good for man to be alone." Then in the next verse he puts Adam in a deep sleep and creates Eve from one of his ribs. What a glorious morning it must have been when Adam awoke, and there stood this beautiful woman. Long, flowing hair, beautiful eyes, plump lips, and the list could go on and on. In other words I am sure when Adam awakened from his deep sleep, he had a childlike, Christmas-morning experience. The only difference was he didn't even have to unwrap the present. He didn't have to wait on Santa Claus. The creator blessed him with this incredible gift.

God placed Eve next to Adam. Ladies and gentlemen, if God realized that "it is not good for man to be alone," why can't we? The reason men and women can't get along is the very fact that we don't appreciate one another. Boris Yeltsin hit the nail on the head when he said, "We don't appreciate what we have until it's gone. Freedom is like that. It's like air. When you have it, you don't notice it."

Love is like that as well. Many of the relationships we are in are falling apart because we neglect the men or women in our lives. God recognized that "it is not good for man to be alone," but for some reason we can't. It is not promised that we will be blessed to be in a relationship, yet many of us act as if this is one of God's decrees. There is no scripture that states God will bless you with a man or a woman.

Understand I am not suggesting you settle for anything that comes across your path. What would have happened to Adam if he settled? That would have meant he chose an animal. Let's just say he chose a lioness to be his better half. Can you imagine that? This beautiful creature was created to live in the jungle and to run wild. The only way Adam would be able to make this relationship work would be to take this animal from her habitat. Not only that but he would have to force her to make the relationship work. In the process of trying to make the lioness love him, Adam would have probably found himself as her midnight snack.

Some of you are making this mistake today. You are wandering around, grumbling, "Whoa is me," but you know your relationship is going no-where fast. In your mind you go back and forth on what you should do even though it is quite evident that it is time for both of you to go your separate ways. I pray that you recognize there is a way out of this nonsense. The sky is the limit for you once you decide to relieve yourself of this heartache. If you stay in the relationship, you face the risk of becoming emotionally eaten up inside.

The beauty of this scripture isn't the fact that God proclaimed that "it is not good for man to be alone." The testimony comes in the second half of the verse. We should give God the honor and the praise because he said, "I shall make him a helpmate opposite him." Many of you have endured painful situations because you didn't know this fact. God made us helpmates opposite us. This part of the scripture doesn't mean that opposites attract. Let's take another look at Rochel Holzkenner's commentary on the words of the

Maharal, Rabbi Judah Lowe. This sixteenth-century man of God from Prague believed that these eight words show us God's "intent of marriage." Admit it: many of you have focused your entire life on finding your soul mate or "the one," and you haven't met him or her. You have been looking for a man or a woman who is the male or female version of you, but I am here to tell you that the word doesn't have that in mind. God doesn't want us looking for Mr. or Mrs. Right. They don't exist; they won't exist, and they never did exist. So please put that idea out of your mind. This second half of the scripture says God created a helpmate opposite Adam. So why wouldn't he do that for us?

What is so important about having a man or a woman opposite you? Well, I am glad you asked. Webster's dictionary defines opposite as "a word that expresses a meaning opposed to the meaning of another word." Another definition states that the word means "being the other of two complementary or mutually exclusive things." Note the words of the sixteenth-century rabbi. He wrote, "A person can be a helpmate to his parents, for example, but shouldn't ever stand to oppose them. But a woman, who is of equal value and importance to a man, will help him and oppose him."

The statement of the rabbi of Prague and the definition go hand and hand together to explain the essence of a relationship. Problems arise in a relationship whenever we find ourselves with a yes-man or a yes-woman. This was never God's intention. Notice in the scripture God created "a helpmate opposite him." He didn't make an individual who was just supposed to follow Adam's will. He crafted a woman who was equal in value. That means, ladies, you have a right to sit at the table. Fellas, that means you have the right to come sit at the table. The scripture didn't say God made a woman who made equal money to him. God never expressed the fact that he made a helpmate for a woman who would be the sole provider. He said, "I shall create a helpmate opposite him." So what am I getting at?

God created a helpmate who was equal in value to Adam but opposite him, to keep him sharp. As the saying goes, iron sharpens iron, right? Having a

161

yes-man or yes-woman in your corner doesn't sharpen you. In order to sharpen anything, there has to be some friction. Having a man or woman who is opposite you strengthens you. A lot of men and women fail today because their pride gets in the way. Or their "I know it all" attitude gets in the way.

Understand that being opposite one another doesn't mean there should be shouting matches. It means we all have to come to appreciate our differences. Why must we do that? Well, for starters, the man or woman in your life is supposed to be one of two complementary or mutually exclusive things. I don't know about you, but I want a love that is exclusive. I want that exclusive (no excuse) love Day26 talked about on *Making the Band 4*. Like Willie said, "Life is such a crazy thing/It's never really what it seems."

In the world we live in, most people have the wrong idea about relationships. We all are unconsciously consumed by the misconception that we need a yes-man or a yes-woman. No, ladies and gentlemen, we don't. We need a man or a woman who is opposite us. We need an individual who is going to speak his or her mind. My grandfather always used to say, "Two heads are better than one." Why are we trying to remove one head from the equation?

In Genesis 2:18 we can see that from the beginning, men and women were connected. You wouldn't know that from the way the opposite sexes treat each other nowadays. Rather than embracing our differences, we reject them. Instead of cherishing our unique designs, we denounce them. Our differences are all part of the divine plan because God wanted to create helpmates for us who are opposite us. Realize that Eve and Adam had quite a bit in common. In the word we learn that Adam was created in God's image. God put Adam in a deep sleep and removed a rib from his side. Then God used Adam's rib to make Eve in his own image. As a child I always wondered what was so significant about that rib. As time went on, I learned that the word *rib* in Hebrew can mean "spirit." Could it be that this missing rib explains why men and women are similar yet so different?

Ladies and gentlemen, the arguing, the heartache, and the frustration need to stop now. Stop looking for a man or a woman who is just like you. That is not part of the divine plan. We are supposed to be opposite one another. There is a subtle beauty in this situation, as if the bonding of male and female is God's own special way of balancing man and woman. It is as if when God created Adam, he made him the yin and the yang. Then when he decided that man was not good alone, he put Adam in a deep sleep and removed the yin. To ensure he made a helpmate opposite Adam, he put the yin in Eve.

As noted earlier, God made sure Adam and Eve had a certain commonality. They were both created in his image. Nonetheless there were some fundamental ways in which Eve differed from Adam. She was physically, emotionally, and spiritually different from her mate. She offered things to Adam that he didn't possess, and he did the same for her. As a team each needed what the other offered. As the saying goes, you can't live with them, and you can't live without them. Men might get on your last nerves, ladies. Women might drive you out of your cotton-picking minds, fellas. Yet sooner rather than later, we will take another shot at love.

Speaking of love, Steve Harvey, in his book *Act Like a Lady, Think Like a Man*, states, "Our love isn't like your love" when referring to the differences between men and women. This shouldn't come as a surprise. This goes right along with what the rabbi was explaining. God made sure that men and women balance each other. God created women to provide men with what they don't possess and vice versa for men. I don't agree with the gist of Mr. Harvey's chapter, though. Steve makes it seem like men can't be "humble and smart, fun and romantic, sensitive and gentle, and above all supportive." He acts as if brothers lack the ability to look their women in the eyes and tell them they are beautiful and they complete them while being willing to change the diapers, rub his woman's feet after a bath, and do all these things without her asking. I was fully onboard with the idea that men's and women's love isn't the same, but I am not willing to sign off on that. God did create us to have "helpmate[s] opposite us," but if we love a woman we are going to do our best to make her feel appreciated and loved.

Mr. Harvey, I don't know how you brothers did it in your generation, but the brothers in mine want to love their women wholeheartedly. Maybe not every single one of us sees it that way, but I do. I had the sad honor and privilege of watching an eighteen-year marriage go down the drain. I watched my father love in the manner of which you speak. I watched him proudly profess his love for my mother in public. My father was an entrepreneur, so I even had the opportunity to watch him provide for my mother and me. Lastly my father was a very strong individual, and he protected the family.

But guess what? I can't speak for every woman, but I can speak for my mother. That wasn't enough. There was something else missing in the relationship. I learned from my parents' divorce that men need to man up. Women need to woman up as well. While men profess, provide, and protect for their women, we still need to cater to our women. By the way, for any of you who has read chapter two of Mr. Harvey's book, I am a real man. I just happen to believe that men can offer their women much more then Mr. Harvey's definition of a man's love, which is: "a man's love is different—much more simple, direct, and probably a little harder to come by." I do agree with him when he says you can't expect perfection because that is unrealistic. I know in the case of my woman, she can expect my love to come abundantly. It won't be a little harder to come by. Otherwise it may be a little easier for another man to come by and sweep her off her feet.

I believe relationships are failing because men and women aren't providing for each other's needs. I know where Mr. Harvey is going in his book, but men and women aren't all that different. God created us all in his image. We all have something to bring to the table. A man who loves his woman should not only be willing to profess, provide, and protect. He should also want to prove how deep his love is. On the flip side of that, so should a woman.

I realize sometimes our differences get in the way. I believe the reason men and women can't get along is we aren't willing to appreciate each other's differences. Somewhere along the way, Adam and Eve's descendants saw fit to use their differences against each other. We have forgotten how to hone the incredible power we can possess when we are connected to a man or woman who is opposite us. I am not sure if this can be attributed to insanity or pride, but I am willing to argue that it's the latter. We can't keep doing the same thing and expecting a different result.

Our relationships are falling apart because men and women are living in a sort of fantasy world. God created our mates to be opposite us, yet we seek men or women who aren't. In the midst of this situation, we also get caught up in the shoulda, coulda, woulda philosophy. Albert Einstein said it best: "A man should look for what is and not for what he thinks should be." Men and women have two separate designs, and that's how it will always be. Stop focusing on what you think he or she is supposed to be.

One thing I have learned in my thirty years of life is that no other woman will treat me like my mother. Fellas, I realize your mothers, like mine, are great women, but we can't expect our significant others to be there. Stop thinking your partner is supposed to be like your mother. Ladies, this also goes for you. I know your father treated you like the little princess you are, but that is your father. He's the only man who is going to treat you like that. Stop thinking your man is supposed to act the same. At the same time, stop thinking your man or your woman is supposed to fill a void. Ladies, if you never had a father, it is not your significant other's responsibility to take his place. Stop looking for a daddy, and find the man opposite you. Gentlemen, if you and your mother never had the relationship you thought you deserved, it is not your woman's responsibility to meet this need. Stop looking for a mommy, and find the woman opposite you.

When you truly love someone, you love him or her for his or her good points and even his or her not so good points. The thing we must recognize is that

God gave man and woman the great potential to succeed. The success of a relationship is a testament to how well a man and a woman communicate with one another. My parents' marriage failed because they didn't understand how to communicate with one another. They didn't realize the power of communication. A lot of us suffer from the same issues my mom and dad did. My parents ignored issues and held their tongues when they should have spoken up. When things weren't going right, they could have steered the ship right, but they treated communication as if it was something you kept stored till an emergency arose. John Powell is quoted as saying something I stand behind: "communication works for those who work at it," and he couldn't be any more correct. How do you truly know your significant other unless you have those much-needed conversations?

Why is communication so important? Sociolinguist Debra Tannen stated, "The biggest mistake is believing there is one right way to listen, to talk, to have a conversation, or a relationship." Many of our relationships have failed because of this. We believed our way was the right way, and our significant other's way was the wrong way. This is wrong thinking. Ladies and gentlemen, we each grow as individuals when our opinions are challenged. If that weren't the case, why is school so important? The learning exercises we did as children still benefit us today. Remember all those books we had to read and all those papers we had to write on topics we couldn't have cared less about? Dr. Michael Eric Dyson states, "The books we read as a child shaped the minds we began to think with. And the minds we began to think with shaped the visions and imagination we had for our futures."

This looks like another part of the divine plan. God wants to prosper us all, so he blessed us with individuals who possess the potential to sharpen us. God blessed us with helpmates opposite us to be those men or women who will challenge our viewpoints from time to time and not just for argument's sake. These disagreements in marriages and in relationships can force people to perform the exercise of humility. Through this process men and women can gain maturity, which will allow them to transcend their own subjectivity.

Some of you may still be asking yourselves, "Why is communication so important?" It is a very important factor because it is one of the forces that connects people. For all my gamers out there, understand that communication resembles the HDMI cables that connect your PS4 or your Xbox One to your incredible sixty-inch flat-screen TV. For all of you nongamers, communication resembles a bridge that connects two states separated by a large body of water, which we will call a rift.

This goes out to all my gamers: How do you ever expect to reach level thirty and find the light, legendary exotic and ascendent gear on *Destiny* without ever connecting the two devices together? Clearly you will not be able to display the game on the TV even though the game console and the TV are in working condition. Similarly, how are you ever going to find the love of your life and sustain that love if you can't connect to your significant other's heart?

I can remember my mother always warning me when I was younger never to burn a bridge. Sadly I learned all too well how to burn a bridge before the thought sank into my brain. I learned from the school of hard knocks that many times a bridge collapses due to maintenance issues, and a lot of our relationships are crumbling because of this. We are not maintaining deep and meaningful communications. In my life I did as I have always done, and my bridges went right up in smoke—not because I burned them but because of the words that came out of my mouth. Can you attest to that? Some of you are still dealing with pain because of something you said or something that was said to you quite some time ago. Ten years have passed, and we still suffer the same heartaches because we can't let old hurts go.

Don't let these moot points weigh you down any longer. You are not facing this struggle alone. Noted blogger and marriage coach from across the pond, Stephen Hedger states, "many couples argue about what the other person meant when they said something." Doesn't this sound like a disagreement that you have had with your significant other? If this is the case, a few questions I would like for you to answer for yourself come to mind:

a) Where you surprised at the backlash?

b) Is this something you have grown accustomed to in your relationship?

c) Are you willing to deal with this for the rest of your life?

It has often been said that one of the best kept secrets of any effective relationship is being able to communicate successfully. But what does that look like? That is hard to say. Thanks to the noted blogger and marriage coach from London, England I know what its not supposed to look like. Hedger states, "this process starts when one person listens to their partner's words, and converts those same words into their own meaning, and then repeats back their translation, making their partner responsible for that translation and the new meaning behind it." What seems to be the problem? Well for one, following this ideology could lead your relationship down a slippery slope. Surely you don't want to do that.

Let's go deeper. Wouldn't you agree that assumptions in relationships often tend to create conflict? Acting on speculation alone could very well shake what Hedger calls, "the core of our relationships, trust, respect, integrity, honesty, etc." This *harmless* thought that was acted upon without any proof could leave one of you feeling judged and could crack the very foundation your relationship will be built upon.

The foundation of a relationship can include any number of factors. These can include but are not limited to appreciation, happiness, individual interest, mutual interests, attraction, chemistry, and last but not least, communication. Having a relationship without an ample amount of communication would be like having a house built on a sandy surface rather than on a solid rock. Whenever someone goes to purchase a home, he or she usually has an inspector go and give a full audit of the house on his or her behalf.

Similarly in relationships, I believe that in the early part of the twentieth century, this practice was done by the family during the courtship phase. This courting has completely transformed into the dating process we have today. Since we don't have our families to be the inspectors in our romantic lives, it is important that we assume the role. That is why there is an even larger emphasis on communication than there ever has been before. Not only is communication the bonding agent of the relationship; it also serves as your personal emotional bodyguard. And it serves as the inspector of the individual in whom you are interested. Each and every one of us has a personal responsibility to do our due diligence and open up our information highways for our the people we want in our lives.

So many people believe that a relationship is built on the premise of trial and error. This concept is true, but the question I pose to you is: are you patient enough to do trial and error with everything until you reach a happy medium? If you are a part of the group that can, please feel free to tell my publicists this, and I will make sure that when I am in your city I will come and shake your hand because I am very impressed. I believe that the essence of trial and error is like archery or target practice. While each of these sports is quite doable by everyone, only specialists and the highly talented succeed at them at high levels. While yes, you should try new things, I believe that the concept of communicating removes need for the trial and error method. For the most part we all know what we like, so why don't we give our relationships a chance and communicate about our likes and dislikes? What is the purpose of trying to pin the tail on the donkey blindly when we continue to miss our mark over and over again?

Of course this is quite simplistic, but getting to know someone is simple if both sides are open, honest, trusting, and patient. This is not the Kentucky Derby, so you don't have to come out of the gate with blazing speed.

Whether you want to agree with me or not, it is prudent for an individual to be a lifelong learner. Every day is another opportunity to obtain knowledge about the world we live in, ourselves, and those we love. I learn something new about myself on a regular basis. I test myself daily with P90X training and running through beautiful Cherokee Park in Louisville. Each day that I pass a benchmark, I learn more about my limitations and my strengths. If I am learning new things about myself almost each day, why wouldn't I do my utmost to learn a little more about my significant other and those I care about the most?

In my life I have learned quite a bit from people just through simple conversation. There is no need to interrogate your significant other about everything in his or her life, including those deep-hidden skeletons in his or her closet. On many occasions people become embarrassed or fearful of your reactions, so they climb up in their personal shells for protection, never to unlock those secrets to you again. Patience is very important in a relationship. Patient communication depends on timing. If you and your significant other both master the art of timing, you all will enjoy the thrills of a monogamous relationship. There is no lonelier feeling than being in a relationship with someone and still feeling a sense of being alone. It's hard to rest in a cold bed.

Communication is the key to a healthy relationship, but you must also possess an ample amount of patience and understanding. Have you ever gone to McDonald's or a 7-Eleven® and noticed the warning signs that state the safe is time sensitive? It cannot be opened until the timing mechanism allows it. The same can be said for someone's heart. You can give quite a Herculean effort to crack the safe and steal the contents. But in the end, you will find yourself terribly winded and quite sweaty. Why? The warning proclaims that the safe is not going to open until the timer allows for the door to be unlatched, quite like one's heart.

In *The Conversation*, Hill Harper depicts this point quite well. He explains how important it is for an individual to be emotionally ready to love. I must say that this point opened my eyes. For quite a while, I didn't know what was wrong with me. While I turned the pages of Hill's book, I received the lesson I needed to learn. The book sparked an epiphany. I must say I am indebted to my fraternity brother for his deep insight.

In my life I met a woman who possessed of an ambitious spark that I had never seen, and it was so enticing. She was an investment banker, and she had just received her Juris Doctor in business law from the University of Kentucky. She seemed to have everything she wanted except for a man. She had a five-year-old daughter, but frankly that was not a bother because she seemed to have it all together. Please note that I am strongly placing emphasis on the word *seemed*. In the boardroom and in teleconferences, she commanded respect and demanded results. At home she tried to live by those same rules, and she was unable to get the same results.

After three months of late-night conversations and e-mails, she treated our situation just like she conducted business. She became quite forceful and told me what I should and could do. Even after I explained to her that she was moving light years ahead of me, her demands persisted until finally I had to let her know the gig was up. She then proceeded to interject the M bomb into the conversation even though clearly we weren't even dating. By the way, *the M bomb* is another way of saying marriage.

She began coming off as desperate to me. It was a shame to see such a brilliant, witty, profound woman behave in this manner. She had done her due diligence in school and had achieved academic and professional acclaim, yet she didn't know how to relinquish her reigns and patiently tread into relationship waters. She was doing dives in the deep end while I was wading with floaties in the kiddie pool.

Timing is always important. We each must possess an internal clock that gives us the ability to be patient until the rays of understanding shine down from the heavens. Without this patience our relationships can resemble a pit stop mistake James Courtney and his crew made at a NASCAR race in Winton. Courtney had a wheel changed out, and his crew did not have enough time to secure the wheel on his car before drove off. After he pulled out, his wheel rolled down pit lane, and his car was unable to get back in the race.

NASCAR greats like Dale Earnhardt Jr., Richard Petty, Jeff Gordon, and even five-time Sprint Cup champion Jimmy Johnson all have one thing in common: their understanding with their pit crews. This is due to the communication each has with his crew before, during, and after the event. Again, I can't state it enough: this understanding did not happen overnight, but it did happen over time.

If James Courtney had been patient with his pit crew, he would have bypassed losing a wheel, which in turn would have allowed him to finish the race and possibly win. Yes, I did use the word *possibly* because having great communication and understanding does not ultimately mean you and your significant other will reach the desired goal. Being patient just gives you both the opportunity to reach the finish line.

The essence of patience and understanding reminds me of the NASCAR pace car that comes out during times of caution. Whenever an accident or a torrential downpour occurs, you can expect this car to enter the racetrack. When an incident that can cause harm to the drivers occurs, a yellow caution flag waves, signaling the pace car to join the pack. NASCAR rules state that when the pace car enters the field, every car must follow it. The purpose of this is to set the pace of the race. If a car passes this vehicle during the time of caution, the race team will be disqualified. Some may believe this is not fair, but the reason the pace car even exists is to protect the drivers.

In my life I have had great chemistry with a few women. Unfortunately the relationships sputtered and spun out of control. We were unable to cross the finish line as the checkered flag waved. Sadly, looking back over those past situations, I can say we did cross the finish line, but a caution flag was waving instead. Our relationships were disqualified because we didn't adhere to the rules and follow the pace car. Instead of allowing it to do its job, we rushed full speed ahead even though we needed to slow down. Ladies and gentlemen, in our relationships communication and understanding are the pace car that helps us avoid harm and danger.

The key to unlocking both verbal and nonverbal communication is studying and learning about the other person. It is our responsibility to do our best to learn what makes our significant other tick. We each should know what buttons are good to push, and we should know what buttons to steer clear of. For the most part, we each possess something like a "self-destruct" button. I am not saying we will blow up into smithereens, but I do believe we will become emotionally volatile. Nothing gets under my skin more than someone pushing those buttons, which I deeply dislike being pushed. If we do our due diligence and pay close attention to our significant others, we should be able to sense whether they are bothered by or happy about their nonverbal communication. Both individuals in a relationship need to learn the nuts and bolts of the relationship to ensure optimum levels of happiness.

I firmly believe it is time for someone to dispel the rumor that relationships that possess true love work automatically. Honestly I feel that this statement is one part true and three parts false. The ultimate question I am sure a number of you have is: what is this true love? This is a question I have been dealing with myself. The essence of true love is indefinable, and it is not fair for any of us to touch on such a complex subject in such layman's terms. Referring to it in the English language diminishes its depth. Many of us in the twenty-first century don't even understand the meaning of the word *love*, let alone the meaning of true love. I believe that the English language does us quite the disservice. I must say I deeply appreciate the Greek language for this word alone. The fathers and mothers of democracy had it right in the way they dealt with the concept of love.

In Greek you didn't have to use any adjectives before the word *love* to explain the concept. There weren't any misunderstandings of how deep one's love was for someone. No Greek boys or girls ever had discussions about how much one liked the other, which we refer to as puppy love. How does a puppy really love? I loved the puppies I had as a child till death did us part. The puppies that grew into strong dogs loved me till their last breaths. How is it that we call youthful love puppy love?

Unfortunately in the English language, we use the word *love* as the be all, end all. So when someone has a deep like for an entrée, they state they love it. When a woman gets a beautiful diamond ring from Blue Nile Jewelry, she loves it. And in my life, when a beautiful female loves me, she loves me in a friendly way. What? What is this friendly way?

In Greek there are a number of words to express different meanings of the word *love*. These include but are not limited to *agape, eros, philia,* and *storge*. After reading this book, any female who wants to let me know she loves me as a friend can lose that phrase and just let me know she has deep philia love for me. My heart desires agape love, but I understand this will come when the time is right. Ladies, please don't do it just for me, but do it for the other unsuspecting guys on whom you are about to put the dreaded "friend" label.

Ladies and gentlemen, can we all just get along? Hopefully you will agree with Rodney King. We all *can* get along. It requires a sense of patience and understanding, but we can make it work. It is not going to be a simple feat or something that happens by accident. There has to be a concerted effort to make this team work. Communication is the key that will unlock the love of a lifetime if we are all willing to give a healthy relationship a shot. It is important that a couple works toward achieving an understanding. God has created a man or woman that is meant to be opposite us. From time to time, there will be disputes, but in the end, with some understanding, the relationship will come out stronger. Each individual will come out a little bit wiser.

Like · Comment · Share

9

Make It Last Forever

Richard Rowland Jr.

We all know that the word *commitment* makes both men and women cringe. Both sexes seem to have an issue with commitment. "Men and women must learn that wise commitments do not bind us; they free us" (Harper, 111). To the immature, *commitment* is a very scary word because it is viewed as bondage. But to the mature, it is the equivalent of freedom because it bestows true happiness that cannot be taken away. Are long-committed relationships outdated? Please answer yes or no and explain why.

Like · Comment · Share

Comments

Jennifer Good point, Richard, but I've also run across some mature, married folk who committed some awful things outside their unions.

Kamilia Long-committed relationships are just like life. They are what you make them. I was raised on the belief that real love between two people lasts for eternity. Therefore I believe that they are not outdated. However, a friend of mine whose parents divorced when she was younger now believes in open relationships. As a matter of fact, she's bisexual as well. Therefore she does not believe in the ideal of monogamy anymore. Her new lifestyle is something she was taught and now has rationalized into existence via the 'net and television. These mediums have changed her perception of what a real relationship is. You have to maintain the meaning and value of what a relationship was in yesteryear. The values we bestow on our children are indeed the values they will cherish for a lifetime. Therefore, in my opinion, committed relationships are not outdated; however they have become everyone else's fad.

Nakia In today's society it seems that they are outdated. However, to those mature folks who still haven't found their life partners (notice I didn't say soul mates), long-committed relationships are blessings that we pray for. I think it really comes down to the individual. Some of us are committed relationship people; others would rather not settle for one person. {shrug shoulders}

Michael They are, of course, bondage if you're committing yourself to the wrong person. Wrong being defined as someone you are unhappy to be with, don't mesh with, etc. And of course even the mature will fall into a momentary lapse or two when they reminisce about the single life, and their commitment will seem like a ball and chain. But once again this feeling will fade when they realize that what they have is more important than a brief ability to be free with whomever they choose.

Committed relationships are not a fad, so they can't be outdated. The problem (if you see it that way) is that society is more and more open and accepting of short-term relationships, divorce, etc. Committed relationships should stem from 1) willingness to commit, 2) love, and 3) happiness; these things can't be outdated (especially real love).

Another problem is that people often feel tied down by their relationships because they see others (friends, movies, etc.) who move from girl to girl or have crazy fun times being single. What most men don't think about is that if they weren't a playboy before their relationship started, they won't be one if they end it. They will just be alone, waiting for the opportunity they sought by getting out of their committed relationship.

Kamilia Michael, m*esh,* as defined by most Christian folks, is considered to be "equally yoked." Therefore if you chose to use such negative words as *bondage*, it will be a tumultuous relationship from jump. Yes, I said from jump. However, I agree with the second paragraph.

PS, I think men have too many darn choices now days. You all really believe that you don't have to settle down. Women are coming at you from all corners, and they don't care if you are in a relationship or not, so we as women set the bar and make it easy for you guys to do whatever you want to do. Understand I fully acknowledge the female role in this dynamic.

Howard They're not outdated; it's just hard to find the ingredients for them. People are being raised with different views, experiences, and values. We each need to learn where to find the appropriate ingredients or continue missing out on real love. In the end if you don't find the ingredients of happiness, you will always be dealing with something. My strategy is to do something fulfilling as a career, something where if that is all I do I'll be fine. As soon as I am fine with me, I hope to meet someone with the same interests and views, and she'll be fine with herself too. This will ensure there will be no pressure on either of us.

Kasandra Everybody is too busy believing that the grass is greener on the other side. This is why I think that committed relationships are outdated.

Like · Comment · Share

Richard Rowland Jr.

If everyone is thinking the grass is greener on the other side, how does that mean committed relationships are outdated? Could it be people these days are selfish and only care about number one, so we move around like romantic nomads, going from relationship to relationship, leaching off people's hearts?

Kasandra It's a sad fact, but it is very true, Richard. People stay committed until things go wrong or one's true self is revealed; either way it goes, people are fleeing from their commitments. The reason people are fleeing is they are just too lazy to work on their problems. I have given up on relationships because of all of the lying and cheating I see in so-called committed relationships. It's a wonder that anybody gets married nowadays. A lot of couples seem to just accept the mess, and I can't live with that. What is a woman to do? Stay in a relationship that's not working or leave that relationship and get in another one that doesn't work?

Michael Kasandra, they are not outdated. Commitment will never be outdated. However, the process that gets people there (courting) has changed somewhat drastically since back in the day (i.e., skipping getting to know someone, going straight to having sex, etc.).

Kasandra Michael, you have a point. The problem is that the cookie stock has plummeted. The market is now saturated with gold diggers who will stoop down low enough just to accept a blunt or even a beer. It's sad. A woman can't get a decent dinner without a man getting an attitude because he is expecting something in return. You know what I am talking about too. That is a shame. That is why I request two checks when I go on a date. No one is going to expect me to do anything just because he bought me something. I'm not that easy.

Simone Some people do play that game—i.e., "buy me dinner, and you can cop a feel," but that should never ever be assumed. I agree with you, Kasandra. My friend calls these people "half hoes." I think that the game, if you call it that, is diluted by people who think they are entitled to something, and I am speaking about both men and women. The whole purpose of going on a date is to see if you like the person and you want to get to know them better. This isn't the time to try to get something out of it for free. However you choose to approach your dates is on you.

Like · Comment · Share

Richard Rowland Jr.

Kasandra, would your attitude change if you met a good guy? Will you make him suffer because someone else didn't step up to the plate?

Kasandra Richard, I won't make a good man suffer because of something another man did to me. I have dated a couple of nice men, but my female intuition is in full effect. There are no second chances with me anymore because I am so cutthroat now. If I feel like a man is lying to me, I am through with the relationship at that instant. I will never give another man the opportunity to lie or mistreat me. I will be all right all by myself because I love me. Lies are the gateway to infidelity.

Simone Kasandra, I don't think that you are being fair at all when you say, "All I need is to feel like you are lying to me for me to end the relationship." What if the person you're interested in doesn't want to answer a question because he is trying to keep something that is a very painful memory away from the first date? Keeping the conversation first-date appropriate is the key to having a second date, right?

Kasandra Simone, God gave me the intuition that I have. I used to ignore this intuition I have, and I won't ignore it anymore. I'm just not going to settle anymore. I just want a man to be honest with me. Is that too much to ask?

Like · Comment · Share

Richard Rowland Jr.

No, Kasandra, that isn't too much to ask. You have to understand that good men do exist. You can't continue to treat each and every man like he is the jerk who mistreated you because that is not fair. I can't answer for every man before me, but I can answer for me, and that is the only one I should be expected to answer for. Is it too much to ask for a fair chance without the bias? You have already decided that we are not going to work out before we even begin.

How would you feel if a man treated you like all the gold diggers before you? You very well maybe an incredible woman, but he can't get past the fact that so and so took him for everything. Now you can't even have a decent first date because so and so keeps coming up. He may not say her name, but he disrespects you like so and so. He has a bit of an attitude like he did with so and so. Is that fair to you? Of course not.

You can't keep looking at every man like that one guy who did you wrong. You have to be open and ready to experience new things. Also look at the men you are choosing. Are they worthy of a good woman? Are they up to par? There are good men around, but you won't find them if you are busy being bitter. You won't find them if you can't let go of the emotional baggage from the guys who did you wrong. Just like it is not too much for you to ask for an honest man, it is not too much for a man to ask for fair treatment. Not every man is a dog. He may have manlike tendencies because he smells like a man, walks like a man, communicates like a man, and looks like a man, but that is because he is a man.

Until you get it in your head that you need to give a man a fair chance, maybe you should just enjoy life alone and continue to work on you. By the way, why do you need a man to buy you a decent dinner? You were talking like you were Mrs. Independent earlier, then you act like you want a man to buy you a dinner. Why does he owe you dinner if you don't give him respect? I know that you are bitter, but you must let the excuses go and give love a shot. Stop lying like you aren't miserable, and change your outlook on mankind and see how that works for you. Maybe pick a different guy who is out of character for you.

Simone And dating isn't necessarily for everyone. Maybe "Living Single" is the chorus of your life right now (you like that throwback?), and if you ever feel like you want to be in a relationship you can switch that track to "I Am Ready for Love" and let the relationship happen naturally. When you find the right person, you will not have to compromise your ideals, but you may be surprised by who you will find if you open your mind to a general set of standards and not a specific person (e.g., six foot one, Harvard lawyer who drives a BMW and has no debt and volunteers at a soup kitchen at the weekends and loves his momma... which is my mom's ideal for me).

Latorria Absolutely not. I think the stability of having a partner in life is a necessity for many—not all, though. I think there are some who could live single forever and be fine. Even the Bible demonstrates that to us. However, the majority of us need to find that person forever. I think it takes maturity. Not to mention a man or woman needs to go through a season of singleness before he or she can be prepared for a relationship. I definitely think long-term commitment is a part of life and a beautiful thing. Of course it isn't easy, but I know I want it in my life. It's much easier not to believe in it than to try.

Yahon First and foremost, God has to be the foundation of any relationship if it is intended to last. Secondly, if the person makes you better and motivates you to grow then you will not look at the commitment as bondage but as a partnership. We need to get back to the values that our grandparents and great-grandparents lived by. We have to realize that you have to work at a true partnership, and at times it will not be easy. But if you are truly committed to one another, you will withstand anything.

Darra Commitment is not outdated. I believe that most want commitment. What's unfortunately becoming outdated is humility. It seems that our generation of twenty-five to thirty-five-year-olds is struck with the "I am the ish" aka "I am a celebrity" disease. Everybody wants to be a celebrity for some odd reason, which makes men always think they can do better because the women who care about them may not be what society categorizes as the physical dime piece or trophy wife. And women do the same thing, but it usually is in a different way. Women try to gain celebrity status by choosing the guy who is flashy or arrogant or who makes the most money. Then they give the humble guy the run around. Not realizing that arrogance is a clear red flag and a sign of insecurity. This can destroy commitment in a relationship.

I am sorry, fellas, but times have changed. Most women today don't come with aprons, pots, and pans in their hands. For the most part, they are not virgins. They all don't look like Beyoncé and have the best flowing roller wrap that you have ever seen. With that said, there are good modern women who have values and have blossomed into relationship material through modern-day trials and tribulations. Times change; we all have to learn to mix modern common sense with old school values. So although she may not be what your grandparents may have considered relationship material, remember to mix the old school values with a little modern day common sense. I am sure that our grandparents wouldn't have been considered relationship material to the generations before them.

I am not saying be committed to someone who you are not attracted to, doesn't want to cook, is unfaithful, or is a bum who doesn't work. All I am saying is when you find someone who is good enough, don't ask for more because you are lucky to find a good person who actually cares about your imperfect self, and that in itself is a blessing that should be cherished. Just work on improving the relationship you have. Commitment means working together and helping each other improve. Both people in the couple must try to be better each day. You have to try to improve. It seems that people are so arrogant, and when they have someone who cares about them they don't see them as a blessing; they take them for granted. They take it as "oh, they must like me because I am the ish!"

How about start choosing your potential mates based on who you feel comfortable with and who you personally are attracted to? Not what your peers think, not what your grandparents think, and not based on who looks good to show off on your Facebook page. The truth is there is a 99 percent chance that you are not famous and are not even remotely close to perfect and never will be. Why choose like someone famous, as if you have the pick of the litter? If you choose like a celebrity, this means you are only picking based on the superficial things, and you will break up just as frequently as the real celebrities do. Superficial qualities do not make a relationship solid, so when times get tough the relationship will be over, and you will be with a new beauty or stud every two months, just like the TV stars. And this is not a good look.

This is not a good look because I have heard many people literally brag about how many fine women they have dated or how many men with money they have dated. I say people need to humble themselves. Guys, flush the tantalizing, eligible bachelor Taye Diggs', Brian McKnight's, Denzel's, and Will Smith's (or whichever other celebrities' many of you fellas attempt to mimic and most of the time fail horribly at doing so) images down the toilet. Ladies, rinse the Beyoncé, Jada Pinkett, Nicki Minaj, "I am a dime piece" nonsense down the drain because you are not any of those people and never will be. If you pride yourself on being a dime piece, you should be talking about your inner beauty.

Even though we are not celebrities, we all can be good, loving husbands and wives who may not have every material thing but have the most valuable thing in the world. What is that thing? It is incredible love and commitment. Humble yourself because when it all comes down to it, what really matters in life are the simple things and not the extravagant. It doesn't matter what your peers think. If you find someone who is good enough for you personally, commit and sit down somewhere.

Last but not least, I also see in this discussion that there is a lot of talk about women having baggage. A point that I want to make is that there are just as many men who carry baggage. I have met plenty of brothers who haven't healed up and thought I was going to do them the same way the last woman did. Also many men fear a successful and confident woman who has a smile on her face. I find this ironic because so many men claim to want a woman who is carefree and healed from the past, but when they are faced with a woman like this they don't know what to do. It seems like the more confident and humble you are, the more guys fear the commitment. Maybe they fear that they will get too attached to you, and if you turn sour on them they will get hurt again. I am not sure, but men can be just as bad as women as far as assuming that the next woman is going to do them wrong. I know this from my experiences and the experiences of other good women. People are extremely afraid to get hurt. We can't just focus on this like it is a female problem.

Like · Comment · Share

Richard Rowland Jr.

Are monogamous relationships outdated? Is trying to make love last forever asking too much? While my heart yells no, conventional wisdom says yes. Even forty-two-year-old-actress Cameron Diaz agrees. She is quoted in the *Sydney Morning Herald* as saying she "doesn't believe in sharing her bed with the same person for her whole life." She added in an interview with German magazine *Bunt*: "Our society tries to make us believe you're ready for love at 18, have to get married, and spend the rest of your life with the same man.

Expletive! That's not the ideal anymore these days." I am sure quite a few of you reading these very words have the same sentiments.

Why aren't monogamous relationships the ideal anymore? Before I can begin to refute Cameron Diaz's statement, I must first get a handle on the reasons why men and women frown upon the idea of commitment nowadays. After several conversations with both men and women, I have realized the reason for society's commitment phobia. Men and women go off the deep end when they hear the very word because they fear the idea of giving up their freedom. Do you agree with this? I know I would if this were the case. Who in their right mind would want to subject themselves to such a situation? No one wants to lose their freedom. We all must relish the fact that we were born with three unalienable rights: life, liberty, and the pursuit of happiness. That is why couples have to communicate. Men and women need to be open and honest with each other. What happens often is people put on facades during relationships. I am a fan of saying what you mean and meaning what you say. In many cases a person says what needs to be said to attract a mate, and then, once the relationship is established, the true man or woman comes out.

What am I getting at? Let's use my life for an example. I had the great opportunity to date a woman who was much younger than I was. She was a beautiful woman inside and out. What I loved about her was she had a lot of spirit. She always had a beautiful smile on her face; she was very confident about life, and she had a head on her shoulders. The thing I loved about her the most was that she had integrity. I knew she would stand behind her word, and that was why I trusted her.

During one of our many conversations, the question of "where do you want to be in the next ten years" entered our dialogue. This young woman, being the honest princess she was, told me she wanted to be finishing up her PhD. As our chat continued, I asked her if she saw herself married with children. She said, "No. I need to get my career in order before I will be ready to start a family."

At that very moment I knew what I needed to do. Staying with this woman would be a waste of time for me because I was interested in starting a family in that ten-year period.

After that conversation the young woman and I continued to be friends, but our romantic relationship ended before it had even started. One of my close friends asked me, "Why I didn't you give this woman a chance?" I told her it was because she didn't see herself having a family in the same time span that I did. My friend then stated something that has stuck with me to this day: "Women may tell you a lot of things, but that doesn't mean it is a definite. We are more flexible than men. If a man says it, you'd better believe he means it. Women will adapt."

I realize my friend, who is a psychologist, can't speak for all women. She was speaking from her experience and the experiences of a few women she knew.

To this day that young woman is working on building her career, and she is nowhere closer to building a relationship than she was when we dated. Imagine if we didn't have that conversation, and I patiently waited for her to realize that she loved me and was ready to start a family. I would have lost my freedom.

What if this scenario were different? What if instead of telling me the truth, she implied she would be willing to be in a relationship? Instead of being upfront with me, let's say she decided to lead me on. Year after year I passed wonderful women who were ready and willing to start families. I bypassed them because I based my future on a lie.

It is going to be very hard to make love last forever when there isn't any love there in the first place. That is why we must have those conversations. We need to know what kind of man or woman we have in our life. It is very important we know what he or she wants out of this life and he or she deserves to know what we want. Not to mention it is critical to know what each of us wants out of a relationship. If he or she loves the single life and wants to have the freedom of a single man or woman, let him or her be single. There are privileges to being single and to being in a relationship. Relationships fail because men and women are selfish. People are consumed by having their cake and eating it too. I know it's cliché, but you know as well as I do that this is true.

Men and women are in committed relationships, but they want to go out and party like rock stars. Like single, no-strings-attached men or women, that is. I am confident that I am not the only person to witness a man or woman who is clearly in a relationship denying it in order to see if he or she's still got it. There is no need for a man or a woman to feel like he or she has been anchored down. Being in a relationship is an option, ladies and gentlemen. At least I would like to think it is. Who wants to make his or her significant other feel tied down? Who wants to be "the old ball and chain"? That sounds like a horrid situation in which to find yourself. This is why communication is always of the utmost importance. Men and women both are emotional creatures, and our attitudes fluctuate day by day.

How does an individual get labeled the "old ball and chain?" If your boyfriend loves gaming, and you take it upon yourself to force him to put up the game console, that could be one way. If she enjoys fine dining and going to the ballet, and you make her accept a six-pack of cold ones while watching a UFC fight in the octagon could be another way. The problem in the relationship isn't that either of the individuals has lost his or her freedom. The issue is they are not accommodating the other's likes. A relationship is a two-way street, and everyone deserves to enjoy the benefits. People lose their freedom in relationships when their partners don't understand that true love is a sacrifice.

People are always quick to say a relationship is about give and take. Frankly I don't agree with this sentiment whatsoever. Relationships are about giving and receiving. Stop treating your significant other like he or she is an old dog that needs to learn how to do a new trick.

What am I getting at? Well, just look at this scenario. We housebreak our puppies so they don't use the bathroom in the house. We scold them when they mess up, and we reward them when they do what we want them to do. Richard, what is wrong with that? My issue isn't that you are rewarding the love of your life for the nice work he or she has done. Showing the man or woman in your life that you appreciate him or her is a very good practice. Don't get me wrong. I am concerned because men and women do things because they have ulterior motives. They do things because they expect to gain things in return. How can anyone ever say they love someone if they are doing things for this person because they will in turn reap the benefits?

Mature men and women realize that true love requires hard work. Authentic love goes beyond this "I scratch your back if you scratch my back" mentality. When you love someone, you are focused to make him or her happy and vice versa. Ladies and gentlemen, there is one thing about love we must all understand: it is not selfish, so quit doing things to get something in return. There is no greater feeling than having someone who does the sweet things he or she does just for the pure enjoyment of watching you be satisfied and happy. Those relationships in which people do this will last longer.

Men and women also have issues with commitment because they are more focused on their other priorities. I am sure I am making an obvious point, but I am going to say this anyway. Love is not to be taken lightly, and a commitment is a priority that requires quite a bit of focus and dedication. You cannot wing a relationship and expect it to work. Committing yourself in mind, body, and soul to another human being sounds like quite the Herculean task, but it's not.

I admit with all the stories of cheating and deceit, it would seem more prudent to stay unattached rather than to allow yourself to get involved with someone. If you do have other commitments that are quite time consuming, maybe you should take care of business first and then think about a relationship. Sometimes in life you can't put your priorities aside; you have to work things out first. I would never suggest you drop out of school for the man or woman you are dating. I would never ask you to leave your ailing parent in need for the possibility for a relationship, and I definitely wouldn't ask you to get into a long-committed relationship that might end in marriage if your credit score is so low that on your credit report it says "ridiculous." A man and a woman have to do what they have to do before they agree to get into a relationship. You will be selfish otherwise. Remember, when you say you love someone, that means you are committing to doing whatever it takes to make him or her happy.

People cringe at the idea of being in a long-committed relationship because they just aren't mature enough for one or ready for it. A lot of you are in the school of belief that age isn't anything but a number. I can remember using this line when I was trying to get an older woman to take me seriously and give me a chance. At one time this was my mantra. Now I don't agree with this statement at all. While age might be just a number, it very well could be an indicator of how an individual views relationships. Sure, an individual between the ages of eighteen and twenty-four desires a healthy and loving relationship like those men and women who are more seasoned. I know at the age of thirty, if I don't want to be sixty years old with kids in high school, I need to make a love connection, get married, and have some babies pretty soon.

Eighteen- to twenty-four-year-olds feel they still have time, and honestly they do. I can remember my younger days, when I had a laundry list of things a woman wanting me to commit had to embody, and now that list has changed. The things I used to value the most I don't anymore. In order to make a long-committed relationship work, both individuals involved must be committed. Everyone involved has to be onboard, or there will be a problem. If everyone is not onboard, the relationship will surely fail, or one or both of the individuals will be miserable.

The reason both men and women are fearful of committing to relationships varies from person to person.. I believe that the largest problem we all have is that we have lost hope. For whatever reason men and women have just taken the Chicken Little approach. Don't you remember Chicken Little? Many of us are mimicking him today. We are running around, hysterically believing that all hope for true love is lost. In your minds the sky is not only falling, but it has already fallen.

For those of you who believe true love is dead, fear not. In some way, somehow, we have to man up and woman up. I hear so many people picking up the mantra that life is what you make it, but I don't hear too many men or women claiming love is what you make it. We must learn to beat our chests with our fists like Kevin Garnett and yell out "anything is possible."

Ladies and gentlemen, we have to understand that 80 percent of a relationship is purely mental while 20 percent is emotional. I am sure I am stepping out on a limb by myself, but please take a moment and just hear my argument. Quite a few relationships have failed because someone thought someone was underappreciating them, someone believed the grass was greener on the other side, or someone just gave up on the idea of being in a relationship, period. I know this might be hard to put your finger on, but just think about it. Is love really enough to drive a relationship? Unfortunately I would have to say no. Love is not enough

This is why it is so important for each of you to believe that your love is worth fighting for. You have to will your relationship to work. Understanding the importance of how people's mind-sets can affect the outcomes of their relationships takes me back to the days when I was pledging my fraternity in my second semester of college. During that time my big brothers gave me some lifelong lessons in the form of poems that I find myself reflecting upon daily. One of my favorites was written by Walter D. Wintle in 1905, a year before my fraternity was founded on the campus of Cornell University. The poem goes by two names: "Thinking" and "The Man Who Thinks He Can." This poem had some very insightful words which I want to share with you.

> If you think you're beaten, you are
> If you think you dare not, you don't
> If you'd like to win, but think you can't
> It's almost a cinch you won't
> If you think you'll lose, you've lost
> For out in the world we find
> Success begins with a fellow's will
> It's all a state of mind
> If you think you're out-classed, you are
> You've got to think high to rise
> You've got to be sure of yourself
> If you ever want to obtain a prize
> Life's battles don't always go
> To the stronger or faster man
> But, soon or later, the man who wins
> Is the man who thinks he can.

Clearly the key to making our love last forever is first to have in our minds that it will last forever. I know it is hard to be positive about relationships when we have far more horror stories than success stories about them. Even with that said, before you get in a relationship you must make sure that you are willing to do what it takes to succeed. No matter how hard it gets, you have to be prepared to go against the status quo. You can't continue having low expectations. We each have to recognize that failure is a part of life. A lot of us lose confidence the first time we make mistakes, but life doesn't work like that.

Wintle's words will hopefully help you overcome your fear of failure. If you doubt your relationship then understand that it won't work. If you think that you and your partner can't make it last forever, it won't. We have to realize that success begins with a man and a woman's wills.

It is important to visualize a successful outcome in anything you do. The great Michael Jordan used mind over matter to become one of the greatest basketball players of all time. This man gave us a wonderful strategy to live by. Jordan explained one time in an interview that he always pictured the basketball going through the hoop before he took the shot. Before he shot his free throws, and even before he shot his game winners, he saw the ball going through the hoop. He also envisioned the hoop was bigger and that he could never miss a shot, so whenever it came time he was willing and ready. Everyone thought it was because he had ice water running in his veins, but the reason he stepped up at times when others defaulted was because he perceived himself winning. This is important for all of us.

If you and your lovely mate want your relationship to work, you both have to envision not only the tuxedo and the white dress but also your cute grand-kids sitting on your laps. The wedding is a very important day, but it lasts only a day (though planning can last for months). I fear that far more people reach for temporary goals, but they are too afraid to step out on a limb and go for it. A wedding is one day, and marriage is for life. I know that weddings are both beautiful and fun, but they do not make or break a happy home. After we jump the broom, unleash the doves, and kiss each other in front of family and friends, we have to make it a point to make it last forever.

I am fully aware that a long-lasting, committed relationship seems like something from prehistoric times, but it can still work today. Each and every person involved must be in tune with himself or herself and with his or her boyfriend, girlfriend, or, most definitely, spouse. Relationships like these are very risky, but the rewards can be immeasurable.

There will come a day in all our lives when we must finally grow up. I know the idea of committing to someone makes you want to cringe, but you don't have to cringe anymore. You know that commitments do not bind you; they truly free you. This will be true if you and your significant other make it a point to work at anything and everything to make your love last forever. No longer will you assume that committed relationships are outdated because you know why most relationships fail.

Like . Comment . Share

10

Superstar

Tiara A young man and a young woman were having a conversation, and this is the dialogue that ensued. "Will you be my superstar?" The guy replied, "Only if I can be your costar." This statement is what makes a relationship successful, right? Marinate on that for a while.

Like · Comment · Share

Comments

Kendall Relationships are like the human body. Sometimes more weight is on one foot. There are times when there is more pressure on one side of the body. With each step we take, our body's balance goes back and forth. Sometimes the right foot takes the lead, and sometimes the left foot takes the lead. In a relationship we are equal, but from time to time one person has to be the stronger of the two.

Derrick In my seventeen-year relationship with my wife, I am the super-star-like Underdog, and she's the female Overcat. Both of us have the same powers and skills, but where I sometimes go at a fast pace she takes it nice and slow. To make your relationship work, it is important to find a happy medium.

Sarah I think that my husband and I are both superstars in our own ways. He's a superstar at some things, and I am a superstar in other ways. Our marriage works well because we are the yins to each other's yangs, and we are in good balance.

Treone I think Ms. Sarah hit the nail on the head. One may shine in one area while the other shines in something else. It's like a movie that has a good comedic actor paired with someone who's good with drama. Both names are on the marquee, and both actors are going to get paid. The same can be said even if both are good in the same area. How would the movie *Life* be if any of those comedians had been a super diva on the set? The trouble comes in when one gets the big head (proud and selfish) and/or thinks that the two are competing. Egos have to be put aside so that the greater good can be accomplished. Be comfortable with whatever role you play, whether it is the main character, a supporting actor, or just a brief cameo. Regardless of this fact, you have to play your part well to ensure the relationship works.

Michael This depends totally on the relationship and the people in it. I've seen successful relationships both ways. Some people want to be the stars, and others are content with being regular in the relationship. There is also the phenomenon of public versus private. In public one person may be the star, but in private the roles are switched. For example, Girl X may be the star in public, catching everyone's attention, etc. At home she loves Guy Y so much that she hangs on his every word and gives him all of her attention, to the exclusion of others.

Erica H. Everyone should shine and be the star in their life. Once we find our mates, it is about creating a unified light.

Erica R. There has to be mutual understanding. Basically your thoughts should be geared toward serving your significant other's needs, and he or she should be focused on serving you. I believe that when this happens, everyone's needs should be met. Issues arise when the couple loses focus on what is important. Whenever a man or woman's needs aren't met, there is more of a likelihood that an argument or a disagreement will occur. I don't think it matters whether either individual or both individuals are superstars. Love conquers all. It doesn't matter if he or she is playing the supportive role or not. I believe if both partners deeply believe in this concept, they will achieve what they desire and a very happy relationship.

Like · Comment · Share

██ **Richard Rowland Jr.**

"Will you be my superstar?" Wouldn't you relish the opportunity to be revered by someone? Not just anybody but the man or woman you love. When I first read this post, I was completely floored by the young man's response to this question. Think about it: who doesn't want to live a little of the good life? Nowadays society is quite star-driven, and it seems everyone wants his or her shot at fifteen minutes of fame. Not to mention we are surrounded by men and women who are all about themselves. This mentality is not conducive to a successful relationship. When two people come together it is important for each of them to understand that there are three parts of the partnership: you, me, and we. The most difficult part of the relationship is learning how to balance all three. It is vital that each partner has the freedom to be able to maintain his or her own identity. Each person must get his or her needs met, and at the same time both individuals must not neglect to nurture the relationship.

One of life's tiny secrets was unveiled when the young man replied, "Only if I can be your costar." What did the young man reveal? Pope John Paul II stated, "Man always travels along precipices. His truest obligation is to keep his balance." And he hit the nail on the head. Our lives are a delicate balance. It is our responsibility to eat a balanced diet, balance our time, and balance our spending, to name a few—or we suffer the consequences. Unhealthy eating habits can lead us on an early journey to the grave. Life is a precious gift, and we should cherish every minute we live.

It is not always an easy feat to make time for everything, but it is important to make time for the things you love. More important, make time for the ones you love. I shouldn't have to say a mumbling word about balancing or spending because the American government taught us how important this is. One more misstep and the United States will find itself in the second Great Depression. If balance is important to our lives, wouldn't you like to think it would be vital to our relationships?

What makes a successful relationship work? I know what you are thinking: *It depends*, right? Well, if you are thinking that, you are partially correct. This sense of balance is a critical component of any relationship. As the saying goes, a relationship should be a balance of two people. One person shouldn't be giving while the other is only taking. Hmmm, this is a very interesting point. Why? This statement goes against Steve Harvey's views. He claims, "Once we've [men] claimed you [women], and you've returned the honor, we're going to start bringing home the bacon. That is our role—our purpose" (Harvey, 24–25). But Mr. Harvey, won't this remove the delicate balance of a relationship?

I understand that "society has told men for millennia that their primary function was to make sure their families were set" (Harvey, 28). My father was born in 1945, and he taught me the same thing. The funny thing is while growing up, I watched my mother financially take care of the family. Not because my father was less of a man but because my father's money had to be reinvested to protect the family business. "Providing for the ones he loved and cared about, whether monetarily or with sweat equity" (Harvey, 29)could have been a part of Dad's DNA, but there was no way for him to battle the new economic climate of the 1990s. He needed Mom to help out financially.

If my parents weren't willing to work together, the family business would have failed, and we would have been one of the many families to experience foreclosure. Surely I don't have to remind anyone that we live in a unique time in our history, when we common men need women to pitch in and help financially. I know Mr. Harvey wouldn't understand this. How could he? The brother makes more money in a year than I will ever see in my lifetime.

To his credit, Mr. Harvey does have a point. Tradition has taught us that a man is supposed to be the provider. Just because society recommends this, it doesn't mean it's right. There once was a time when men and women believed that the world was flat. How's that idea working out for us today? Seen a globe lately? Need I say more?

Mr. Harvey has every right to tell his audience that "the very core of manhood is to be the provider" (Harvey, 25). By no means am I arguing that it is not a man's responsibility to take care of his family because it is. I just take issue with his tone. He makes it seem like it is the man's sole purpose in the relationship to provide. This may sound all well and good, but look at what this attitude has blessed us with. I have two words for you: *Basketball Wives*. If you don't like that example, I have another one for you: *Housewives of Wherever You Want It to Be*. I wouldn't have a problem with these shows if the women on them were bringing more to the table than just their good looks and their attitudes. By the way, before I offend the whole set of these shows, I am not speaking of every woman. I am not going to say any names, but we all know who I am talking about. This is why I have a problem naming men as providers. Now you have women seeking men to provide them with lavish lifestyles when they have the talent and the brains to do it themselves.

If you don't want to take my word for it, please read these words from one of the wisest men to walk this Earth. In his Song of Songs, Solomon wrote these words that his beloved speaks:

> "Tell me, you whom I love
> where you graze your flock
> and where you rest your sheep at midday.
> Why should I be like a veiled woman
> beside the flocks of your friends?
> If you do not know, most beautiful of
> women, follow the tracks of the sheep
> and graze your young goats
> by the tents of the shepherds"
> (Song of Solomon 1:7–8, NIV)

This scripture is a wonderful testimony to the balance that is expected in a relationship. In the text from Song of Solomon, it isn't just the man who is working. The man has a flock of sheep, and the woman has a herd of goats. Both of them are working. This woman isn't interested in the shepherd because of what he has. In the words of Jamie Foxx, "she got her own." She has her stuff together. The brother has his stuff together. That's what makes their relationship balanced.

Pastor Jeffrey A. Johnson Sr., author of *The Song of Solomon*, wrote:

> Too many sisters are waiting in their predicament for some brother to come up on a white horse and pull them up out of poverty, but they'll probably be waiting forever. A man wants the same thing you want in marriage partner. He wants somebody who's got something, or is on her way to becoming something.

And he couldn't be more right. The biblical text shows you that this woman could provide for herself. And if she could do this in a time when men were revered as masters, why can't you do so in a time when women are given far more opportunities?

Thoughts like these make building relationships more difficult than it already is. Trying to achieve what Drake and Alicia Keys called the "unthinkable" is a difficult balancing act. Life coach Brian Tracy explains, "Just as your car runs more smoothly and requires less energy to go faster and farther when the wheels are in perfect alignment, you perform better when your thoughts, feelings, emotions, goals, and values are in balance." Couldn't we say the same thing about a relationship? In the words of President Barack Obama, "Yes, we can!" A relationship performs better when two people's beliefs, spirits, passions, objectives, and principles are in tune with each other.

We have already extensively discussed the significance of being in tune with your star player. When this young man responded to the question "will you be my superstar?" with "only if I can be your costar," he was expressing how in tune he was with his own star player. Ladies and gentlemen, in case you forgot this part of our discussion in chapter six, let me give you a reminder. Being in tune with your star player doesn't give you the excuse to be a diva or a prima donna. Unfortunately this self-centered attitude seems to be at an all-time high. We can't allow ourselves to fall into the same trap that so many have already stumbled upon. Sooner rather than later, every man and woman must learn to drop the "I" concept and embrace the "we" principle—that is if both he and she want their relationship to accomplish what many deem the impossible.

Why is it essential for men and women to adopt the "we" principle? Embracing a team concept is a fundamental part of any successful relationship. If you don't make a good teammate, guess what? You don't make a good mate either. Understand that being a good teammate doesn't mean you play as well as LeBron James, Aaron Rogers, or Maya Moore. Being a team player means you are willing to embrace the spirit of Bumblebee, Scottie Pippen, and last but not least Michelle Obama. Nowadays it seems men and women have overlooked this necessary facet of a healthy, happy, loving partnership.

The problem may be that men and women don't understand how to unleash their inner team players. I learned the importance of "we" as opposed to "I" while playing sports and pledging my fraternity. Playing for an athletic team is like being in a relationship. Each team usually has the superstar or the superstars, the supporting cast, and its adoring fans. The same can be said for a couple. It can be made up of two costars and a supporting cast that includes family and friends. The only way teams with more than one superstar can expect to win is if they pitch their egos to the side. Ladies and gentlemen, if we want our love to be successful we have to kick our selfishness to the curb. In some way, somehow, you and your special someone have to remove pride from the equation in order for the greater good to succeed. This is yet another example of how communication is a must.

The greatest sports teams all have one thing in common: each team was able to reach its level of success because it honored each player's individuality while working toward the group's success. An example of this was when the Chicago Bulls signed bad boy Dennis Rodman, and all the analysts doubted it would be a marriage made in heaven, but they were wrong. Dennis Rodman was a special character. This brother published an autobiography called *Bad as I Wanna Be*. During one of his book signings, he had the audacity to show up wearing women's clothing. During the season he appeared at the Chicago Bulls games with green hair, bright canary-yellow hair, and red hair that surrounded the black Bulls emblem. In his first season in Chicago, he was suspended for eleven games because he head butted a referee. I admit that Rodman's antics were off the wall, and I would never expect anyone to accept his attention-grabbing behavior, but somehow the Bulls were able to let Rodman be himself while winning three championships in a row. There were problems along the way, but in the end Jordan, Pippen, and Rodman found a way to share the stage and celebrate success together. How did they accomplish this feat? They removed their pride from the equation and worked toward a common goal, as we all should.

I hear so many self-proclaimed advisors instructing men and women to let go of their egos. People throw the word *ego* around, as if they know what they are talking about. Do they know what they are talking about? I can answer this in a single word: no. What comes to mind when you hear the word *ego*? Admit it: when you hear it you visualize obnoxious men and women who can't seem to talk enough about themselves. In your mind you find yourself strumming through images of T.I., Naomi Campbell, and Charlie Sheen. It's hard not to do this. I get it. You believe these people think they have tiger blood running through their veins, and they believe that without a doubt that they are winning. We have transformed the word that Sigmund Freud coined into a dirty, three-letter word. Do I really have a dirty mouth if I believe I have an ego? Will the blond woman from the Orbitz gum commercial show up and hand me a piece to clean my dirty mouth? Surely not.

For some reason people have very negative ideas when it comes to the word *ego*. However, we should not look down upon this word. Rather we should applaud individuals with egos. What is an ego? It's is a person's self-esteem and the way he or she views himself or herself. Remember, we should appreciate a man or woman for being in tune with his or her star player. The masses have grabbed their pitchforks and prepared to hunt down and capture the word *ego* dead or alive, but we may want to put a halt to this bloodthirsty mob. You have the wrong man. The culprit is not an individual's ego. The one we seek is pride. An individual's pride is his or her personal view of his or her own importance. I can only imagine what would happen if a man or woman's pride were allowed to run freely in a relationship. In order to make love work, both individuals must dial down their pride. My grandmother always taught me that love is a sacrifice. I still hear her to this day saying, "The truest type of love requires a man and a woman to sacrifice their happiness for the happiness of the one they love."

Lupe Fiasco and Matthew Santos said it best on the track "Superstar":

If you are what you say you are, a superstar
Then have no fear, the camera is here
And the microphone's on
And they wanna know oh, oh, oh
If you are what you say you are, a superstar
Then have no fear, the crowd is here
And the lights are on
And they wanna show oh, oh, oh yeah

I believe the essence of this song speaks volumes about letting your pride go. How many of you have ever gotten caught up in your own hype? If we would all be honest, we would agree that there have been times in our lives when we acted like superstars. I can remember mine like it was yesterday. Sometimes I just laugh and shake my head. I used to be so young and dumb, and I acted as if I could do no wrong. In my own eyes, I was the man, the myth, and the legend. I believed that every woman wanted an intelligent, handsome member of my fraternity. I had the game down pat, and I tried to run it across any young lady who wanted to hear it.

In my mind I was so big and bad, I didn't think there were any women who didn't want to hear it. I learned swiftly that I was not a superstar. The problem was I found myself like my favorite line from "Superstar": "Wanna believe my own hype, but it's too untrue." In the beginning you couldn't tell me that; I had to find out the hard way.

I realize in some of your minds, this may seem like a contradiction. Please follow me for a moment. There is something on which I want us to agree. I am not trying to tell anyone not to be in tune with his or her star player. I believe every man and every woman should be his or her own cheerleader. We all have to be able to pump our confidence up. Along with that, it is important to recognize both the good as well as the bad. By the way, this is a delicate balance. There is nothing wrong with you having a high regard for yourself. I applaud anyone for that. Before you can love anyone else, you have to love yourself. The problem arises when you overdo it and start thinking you are better than everyone else. I don't take issue with you noticing your faults. I get concerned when people focus only on their faults.

Now it is time to delve deep into the lyrics of "Superstar." In the opening lines of the song, Matthew Santos sings, "If you are what you say you are, a superstar." What do you think he is getting at? Take a moment and think back on a man or woman you met who claimed he or she was all that. After the initial conversation, you swore up and down he or she had to have it going on. This man or woman proclaimed he or she was a different kind of man or woman. "I assure you that you can trust me," he or she said.

Have you ever heard this before? Did you trust this man or this woman only to find out he or she wasn't who he or she said he or she was? In the end, he or she did the same things ole boy or ole girl used to do. Sometimes men and women get caught up in their own hype and oversell themselves. Sadly, I have done this a time or two. I would like to take this opportunity to apologize to all of the women I ever did this to. There is nothing wrong with possessing a strong sense of self, but the problem occurs when you cross the bridge of humility into Conceitedville.

The issue is not that you hold yourself in high regard. It is the fact that your view of yourself isn't realistic. It is one thing to think one way about your image if it matches everyone else's view. And it is another when you think one way and everyone else sees you in a different light. I already know that not everyone's opinion is important, but I would like to think the views of your loved ones and the people you care about matter.

As the chorus of the song continues, it warns, "Have no fear, the camera is here/And the microphone's on/And they wanna show." This shouldn't come as a surprise. One thing we all must understand is if we are going to talk a big game, we need to be prepared to back it up. There will come a day when we will have to put up or shut up. If you happen to be a graduate of the Chicagoan Institute of Kanye West University, please come back down to planet Earth. I realize this might be a difficult task, but you need to find a way to join the rest of us.

Ladies and gentlemen, I honestly have no problem with an iota of confidence, but I beware individuals with that Hollywood confidence. The last time I checked, when the cameras and microphones are near and the lights are on, they are just fine. Unfortunately, when the cameras aren't rolling, we see the problems. Lindsey Lohan, Charlie Sheen, Mel Gibson, and O. J. Simpson are a few examples of this. Need I say more? None of us smells like roses, and if you are one of those individuals who believe you do, understand roses really don't smell too good.

If that doesn't paint a picture for you, I am going to have to go to the notes I received from Andre 3000. In his song "Roses," he sings, "I know you'd like to think your stuff don't stank/But lean a little bit closer/See that roses really smell like poo-oo-ooo/Yeah, roses really smell like poo-oo-ooo." Having your confidence on level ten is very attractive. The problem arises when you think too highly of yourself. Just another example of how important balance is in our lives and our relationships.

Balance in a relationship is dynamic. It changes from moment to moment. Trying to love someone unconditionally is a difficult balancing act. We all have to make efforts to ensure our thoughts, feelings, emotions, goals, and values are in alignment with our significant others'. Many times relationships fall apart because men and women misunderstand what being united with someone means. It doesn't mean uniformity. It means togetherness. In the text of Song of Solomon 1:7–8, we read that we all bring something to the table. An important fact is we have to learn to appreciate the special men or women in our lives. Not to mention we need to appreciate ourselves for all of our good points and our bad. You are a superstar in your own right, and so am I. Since this is the case, that means we all must be willing to be someone's costar. Learn to practice some humility, and reap the benefits with the man or woman of your dreams.

Like . Comment . Share

ACKNOWLEDGEMENTS

✤

In the highest sense of gratitude, I presume to offer up my most sincere thanks to the Almighty, the Creator, and Preserver for so many great favors and blessings.

Lauren Hill once said that "everything we do should be a result of our gratitude for what God has done for us," and as the Almighty helps me bring my first book to a close, I would like to acknowledge all of those men and women whose unselfish and dignified actions allowed me to become who I am today. I may not be where I want to be, but I am grateful because I am not where I used to be.

Since my book dealt with the numerous conversations I had on Facebook I guess it was appropriate that I entitled my book *Facebook Memoirs*. Through some very formal and some not so formal dialogues, I learned a great deal from so many friends and colleagues about the subjects discussed in this work. I want to take this time to recognize all of my family, friends, colleagues, and fraternity brothers who helped me expound upon my ideas, and gave me new perspectives and concepts to think about during the early versions of the book. They all offered constructive, encouraging, and helpful criticism to push my goal and vision forward. I deeply appreciate them for not allowing me to disassociate myself from the issues, and pushed me to take a risk and to be open and honest about my own relationship story. This work has been a very extraordinary piece of teamwork, and I deeply thank all of you for your help.

This project could not have been done without my very insightful friend Ms. Voijai McClellon and all of her kind words and commitment with this book. To my intellectual and understanding friend, Dionna Owens Wilson, for her outstanding work and support, thank you. To my brother and close friend,

Ernest Camel III, thank you for your talents and being there when I needed a sounding board.

To Christina Powell, thank you for being a great friend and contributing your thoughts, experiences, and views to this book. To my analytical and inquisitive friend, Jasmine Mayfield, for her in-depth views on relationships and playing the devil's advocate at times. And to Shelly Strickland, for taking the time to offer her deep insight. I learned quite a bit from you and James during our college days, and I am happy to say I still am. You two have a very beautiful family that everyone could learn from.

A very special thanks to my mentor, Mrs. Julia Roystons, and the staff at BK Royston publishing for their undying support. Without you my project would not have had the opportunity to be a success. And to Candace Renee Smith and the staff of *Outline:Every Writer's Resource* I applaud you for your great work. You took on the daunting task of editing my work and you did it with flying colors.

A very heartfelt thanks goes to my mother, Emma Lee Bender, for your undying love and great support on all things that I have done and plan on doing in the future. I would say thank you, but the words wouldn't be enough to show you how much I appreciate you.

I can't leave out the gratitude that I have for the staff at Createspace. You guys made this project exciting to work on. There is a lot that goes on behind the scenes when one wants to publish a book, but you guys helped me each step of the way. Thank you to the editor, the on the phone staff, the interior and cover designers. You guys ROCK!

And last but not least, thanks to Him from whence cometh my help- without the will, love, and support from my Creator- neither this creation nor I would exist.

Peace, love, blessings, and happiness to all.

REFERENCES

❧

1. Barker, Camilla. 2005. "The Lost Art of Listening." *Article Alley*, January 1. Accessed July 4, 2013. http://tirode2art.wordpress.com/2013/03/08/the-lost-art-of-listening/

2. Barash, David and Judith Eve Lipton. 2001. *Myth of Monogamy: Fidelity and Infidelity in Animals and People*. New York: Henry Holt and Company.

3. Boyz II Men. "Say Good-bye to Yesterday." *Coolyhighharmony*. Motown, 1991. CD.

4. Boyz II Men. "Water Runs Dry." *II*. Motown, 1995. CD.

5. Chris Brown. "Say Goodbye." *Chris Brown*. Jive, 2005. CD.

6. Crane, Dr. George W. 1946. *Psychology Applied*. Chicago: Hopkins Syndicate.

7. DeBarge. 1984. "Love Me in a Special Way." *In a Special Way*. Gordy. (CD)

8. *Diary of a Tired Black Man*. Dir. Tim Alexander. Perf. Tim Alexander, Paula Lema, Jimmy Jean-Louis. Screen Time Films, 2008. DVD.

9. *Diary of a Mad Black Woman*. Dir. Darren Grant. Perf. Kimberly Elise, Steve Harris, and Tyler Perry. Lions Gate, 2005. DVD.

10. *Fireproof*. Dir. Alex Kendrick. Perf. Erin Bethea, Ken Bevel, Kirk Cameron. Sherwood Pictures, 2008. DVD.

11. Haq, Dr. Muhammad Wasif. 2010. "Small Talk: This Time shall Pass Too." *Cool Blues Consortium of Articles*. n.p. n.d., October 1.

12. Harper, Hill. 2009. *The Conversation*. New York: Gotham Books.

13. Harvey, Steve, and Dennene Millner. 2009. *Act Like a Lady, Think Like a Man*. New York: Harper Collins.

14. Hedger, Stephen. 2010. "Why Assumptions Can Harm Relationships." September 30. Accessed November 24, 2014. http://www.stephenhedger.com/relationships/why-assumptions-harm-relationships/.

15. Holzkenner, Rochel. 2009. "Why Can't We Get Along." *The Jewish Woman*, November 9. Accessed August 4, 2010. http:chabad.org/thejewishwoman.

16. *Inception*. Dir. Christopher Nolan. Perf. Leonardo DiCaprio, Joseph Gordon-Levitt, and Ellen Page. Warner Brothers, 2010. Film.

17. Jackson 5. "ABC." *ABC*. Motown, 1970. Vinyl.

18. Johnson Sr., Jeffrey A. 2007. *The Song of Solomon*. Indianapolis: Xulon Press.

19. Johnny Lee. "Looking For Love." *Urban Cowboy Soundtrack*. Full Moon, 1980. CD.

20. Kelly Price. "Tired." *Kelly*. Sang Girl/My Block, 2011. CD.

21. Kennedy, Jon. 2009. "Why We Cheat." *Travis Online Magazine*, February 10. Accessed March 9, 2011. http://travismagazine.wordpress.com/2009/02/10/why-we-cheat-the-8020-rule/.

22. Kirschner, Dr. Diana. 2010. "Aha! Understanding the Mind Games Men Play." *Today Health*, February 19. Accessed March 19, 2011. http:today.msnbc.com/id/35461729/ns/today-relationships.

23. Ludy, Eric, and Leslie Ludy. 1999. *When God Writes Your Love Story*. Sisters, OR: Loyal Publishing, Inc.

24. Lupe Fiasco. "Superstar." *The Cool*. Atlantic, 2007. CD.

25. Marsha Ambrosius. "Some Type of Way." *Late Night and Early Mornings*. J, 2010. CD.

26. *Men in Black*. Dir. Barry Sonenfield. Perf. Tommy Lee Jones, Will Smith. Columbia Pictures, 1997. Film.

27. Moon, Dr. W. Jay. 2011. *African Proverbs: Stepping Stones within Oral Cultures*. n.p, n.d., September 11. Accessed March 9, 2014. https://oralitystrategies.org/resources.cfm?id=279

28. Nichols, John G. 2000. "Following Instructions." *A Better Hope*, June. Accessed November 11, 2014. http://www.abetterhope.com/victory/instructions.html.

29. Outkast. "Roses." *Speakerboxxx/The Love Below*. LaFace, 2003. CD.

30. Raheem DeVaughn. "Customer." *The Love Experience*. Jive, 2008. CD.

31. Robert Kelly. "When a Woman's Fed Up." *R*. Jive, 1998. CD.

32. Rudov, Mark H. 2004. "Can Men and Women Really Get Along? " *Get Ready for Love*, November, 8. Accessed November 11, 2014. http://www.getreadyforlove.com/love-links/lsrudovcanmenandwomenreallygetalo.htm.

REFERENCES

33. Schwartz, David J. 2007. *The Magic of Thinking Big*. New York: Fireside.

34. Subway and 702. "This Lil Game We Play." *Good Times*. Motown, 1994. CD.

35. Tamia Hill. "Stranger in My House." *NU Day*. Warner Brothers, 2001. CD.

36. Tamia Hill. "Almost." *Between Friends*. Image, 2006. CD.

37. Teddy Pendergrass. "Love TKO." *TP*. Philadelphia International Records, 1980. Vinyl.

38. *The Green Mile*. Dir. Frank Darabont. Perf. Michael Clark Duncan, Tom Hanks, and Bonnie Hunt. Warner Brothers, 1999. Film.

39. Walsch, Neale Donald. 1995. *ReCreating YOURSELF*. Ashland, OR: Millennium Legacies, Inc.

40. Wand, Jeffrey A. 2010. *Knock and the Door Will Open*. New York: Atria.

41. "The Checklist." *What Chilli Wants*. VH1. Atlanta. 13 April, 2010. Television.

42. *Why Did I Get Married?* Dir. Tyler Perry. Perf. Janet, Jackson, Richard T. Jones, Sharon Leal, Tyler Perry, Tasha Smith, Jill Scott, Michael Jai White, and Malik Yoba. Lions Gate, 2007. Film.

43. *Why Did I Get Married Too?* Dir. Tyler Perry. Perf. Janet Jackson, Richard T. Jones, Sharon Leal, Tyler Perry, Tasha Smith, Jill Scott, Michael Jai White, and Malik Yoba. Lions Gate, 2010. Film.

44. Xscape. "Softest Place on Earth." *Traces of My Lipsick*. So So Def, 1998. CD.

45. *You've Got Mail*. Dir. Nora Ephron. Perf. Tom Hanks and Meg Ryan. Warner Brothers, 1998. Film.